HELL WEEK
& BEYOND

THE MAKING OF A
NAVY SEAL

SCOTT McEWEN

CENTER
STREET

NASHVILLE • NEW YORK

Center Street
Hachette Book Group
1290 Avenue of the Americas, New York, NY 10104
centerstreet.com
twitter.com/centerstreet

First Edition: May 2021

Center Street is a division of Hachette Book Group, Inc. The Center
Street name and logo are trademarks of Hachette Book Group, Inc.

The publisher is not responsible for websites (or their content) that are
not owned by the publisher.

Library of Congress Control Number: 2021935539

ISBNs: 978-1-5460-8497-6 (hardcover), 978-1-5460-8495-2 (ebook)

Printed in the United States of America

LSC-C

Printing 1, 2021

CONTENTS

PART IV
The End Is a Mirage 191

INTRODUCTION

MY HARDEST TIME

We will all go to hell at some point. Some of us are there now. If you want to survive, learn from the SEALs.

n the mid- to late 2000s, two major wars raged on the far side of the world, one in the craggy mountains and valleys of Afghanistan, and the other on the urban streets of Iraq, in cities like Fallujah, Baghdad, and Ramadi. These wars were fought between the militaries of Western nations against hordes of terrorists and deranged Muslim extremists hell-bent on destroying the world by waging no-holds-barred guerrilla-style combat, using shit-caked IUDs (bombs literally painted with human fecal matter to cause infection after injury), suicide vests wrapped around impressionable teenagers, and human shields made up of women and children. The cowardly zealots used these deplorable tactics not to win battles, but to inflict maximum suffering and devastation on the United States of America and her allies, as we tried desperately to end the suffering of the populations of nations held hostage. U.S. forces, our men and women, took on the lion's share of the fighting, along with that of the dead and the wounded. Our sons and daughters gave up life and limb, village by village and block by block, in an effort to liberate these nations and bring peace to the land. Every week, accounts of U.S. engagements were reported in the media, along with the butcher's bill tallying the shocking loss of American lives. Twenty of the most highly trained U.S. Special Forces fighters died in a single day. It was U.S. Special Forces, especially the Navy SEALs, who fought behind enemy lines, experiencing close-quarters engagements at a level not seen since World War II.

Back in the comfort of our homeland, I *thought* I was going through my own personal hell. My second marriage had ended bitterly and a far more insidious battle with my ex-wife had begun, presumably over custody of our son. Of course, the battle was really about money and revenge. At work, I spent my days in airless courtrooms across the United States stuffed into a monkey suit, downing caffeine to fight off the effects of sleepless nights and hangovers while listening to the clacking of court reporters as I litigated wrongful death cases for deep-pocketed clients, usually in gruesome circumstances.

For example, a van full of intoxicated illegals is hit on a train track and the van's gas tank explodes, tearing six bodies apart and burning them all at once. *I am called in to defend the railroad. I win.* Brakes, which allegedly malfunction one morning when a bank executive is on her way to work and is literally lobotomized when she is flung through the windshield of her car and smashes headfirst into a concrete divider. *I am called in to defend the automaker. I win.* A fire alarm fails to sound in a nursing home and smoke inhalation and flames take lives. *I am called in by the private equity fund that owns the nursing home. And I win.*

I was the legal mercenary who helped big corporations avoid taking massive losses when their products maimed or killed. Killing was better for my clients. The dead don't need lifelong medical attention.

With my life being grim at home and gruesome at work, I felt a burning need to bring light into this world, to give back to our valiant troops fighting real wars overseas. After work I offered pro bono legal advice to local military service members. I just wanted—no, I needed—to help others, to do something good for good people and perhaps to find redemption for myself.

Since I lived near the Naval Amphibious Base at Coronado Island, California, the home to West Coast–based Navy SEALs and training ground for all of BUD/S (Basic Underwater Demolition/SEAL Training), I was blessed with the honor of offering help to these finest of warfighters. Mostly I advised on civil matters: property issues, bad loans, and the occasional domestic dispute. Ironically, I excelled at helping my clients shore up their lives while mine crumbled underneath me. And the SEALs needed the help. Sadly, many of our military fall victim to unscrupulous lenders and conmen who often prey on military spouses when service members are overseas.

In the fall of 2009, I went to Coronado to meet an active-duty SEAL in a bar. He needed to talk to a lawyer and had heard I could be trusted. A mutual friend, a former Vietnam-era SEAL, named LZ, wanted to introduce us. LZ was more than a warrior of the old school; he was a stone-cold maniac. He had a taste for cheap whiskey, even cheaper Mexican prostitutes, knives, and dangerous situations, and he absolutely despised anything resembling regular old quiet life. Simply stated, if you chose to drink with this man, you were best off bringing bail money. I met LZ when a neighbor recommended him as a jack-of-all-trades—an honest trade he tried his hand at when he ran out of cash. I'd been warned by my neighbor, "He's a very good stonemason...when he shows up."

While sitting at a side table drinking a vodka soda with LZ in a bar that smelled like stale beer and salt air, I saw a man approach our table from behind. Pantera blared from inside the bar out toward the patio where we sat. The man moved light on his feet, silent on stone. Careful to stay out of LZ's sight, he crept up behind him and slipped him into a headlock, saying, "When you gonna finish my patio? I paid you six damn months ago!" LZ could not get a word out. He turned a dark shade of purplish red as the blood was expertly cut off to his brain, and then he passed out. The man gently laid LZ on the floor, then slid his butt into LZ's now empty stool, smiling at me.

"Hey bud, you must be the lawyer LZ suggested I meet," he said, grinning and speaking in an easy Texas drawl. This guy, who had just choked my friend like you might stub out a cigarette, then reached across the table for a handshake and added, "I'm Chris Kyle. How you doin'?"

"Better than LZ, I guess," I told him. A quiet second passed and we both burst out laughing.

Chris had the energy and temperament of a pit bull—strong, quiet, deeply loyal, and serene, almost gentle—yet he was extremely physically powerful, built of solid compact muscle that was coiled tight and ready to rumble. He was someone you could wrestle with, if you wanted or dared. Yet a look in his somewhat sleepy eyes warned you that if you wanted to fuck with him, you'd better be prepared to fight to the death. Instinct told me that if this man, or those who entrusted him to defend them, were threatened, he was capable of killing with ease.

It wasn't just his demeanor that communicated this. Chris had already become an underground legend in the SEAL community. He had a reputation as a serious "pipe hitter," an operator who had seen lots of action and had no problem taking care of business. The most elite warriors whispered about his military record and sniping abilities with reverence and awe. I heard from several reliable sources that Chris had killed more enemy combatants than any sniper in the history of the United States, a record I would later help to officially confirm with the DoD.

After LZ peeled himself off the floor and wove his way unsteadily over to chat up some women hanging out by the dartboard, my conversation with Chris initially focused on his legal trouble. He wanted to know if he had any recourse in a bad business deal—a conman who had swindled the wives of a group of SEALs out of tens of thousands of dollars each. I tried to give him the best advice I knew and offered to help talk to the man and file a lawsuit if it came to that. Chris drifted off, barely interested in the matter.

Reading his body language, I veered the conversation onto horses, hunting, and guns, interests Chris and I shared. Chris had been raised on a Texas ranch and had ridden in rodeos; I had grown up on a remote horse farm in Oregon with a father who had been a World War II pilot. Both of us were experienced and passionate hunters. And we loved guns. "Wanna see something I have in my truck?" Chris asked, and for the first time that night I saw a genuine flash of light in his eyes.

I followed him away from the blaring music and beer smells to the parking lot, where fog from the nearby ocean rolled over the trucks lined up in the lot. Chris hopped up into the back of a Ford F-150, flipped open the lockbox in the back, and pulled out a nickel-plated .45. He removed the magazine, racked the slide, ejected a shell, and handed me the gun. "I carried this with me in Iraq," he said. "On my hip." In the dark lockbox I could see what looked like half a dozen weapons, barrels long and short, stocks and handgrips. Looking at these guns, all military grade and kept and cleaned by the man I would soon learn was the world's deadliest sniper, I knew that these weapons had been used to kill humans. These were the tools of a warrior. He kept them close to his person, always. I took the .45 from him, hefted it in my hand, and sighted it.

"How does it feel?" Chris asked.

"Good and mean," I said.

"Damn right." He grinned and motioned for me to hand back the weapon.

I gave him his gun back. "Want to see mine?"

He looked at me doubtfully. "Sure," he said. "What do you have?"

"Follow me."

We moved over a couple cars to my car, a dusty Porsche 911 with over 100K miles on it and racing suspension—one of the few things of mine I had managed to keep out of my wife's plastic glue-on claws in our divorce. I popped open the trunk in the front, looked around, opened a gun case inside, and pulled out my KelTec semi-auto .223, an assault rifle I often took to the range and kept in case things got hairy—which, given our current crisis in the United States, now seems like a good thing to do.

"Shit," Chris said, looking down at the gun. "What kinda fuckin' lawyer are you?"

"A well-armed one," I joked. "You know how many fuckin' people hate lawyers?"

"Yeah, and I'm one of 'em." Chris laughed. "But you're alright."

Once we had established common interests and values, I believe Chris made a conscious decision to open up and trust me. Over time he began to trust me even more. He trusted my advice, and eventually he would trust me to help him tell the story of his life, an act that would to some degree make him a marked man. Should he have made the decision to chronicle his life and become famous? How many times had those who set themselves on a path to fame only realized later that the "fame" was the reason for their ultimate destruction? Gandhi, Martin Luther King, JFK, RFK, et cetera, et cetera. I could go on, but one gets the point. History teaches us that the greater the fame, the greater the exposure to craziness.

As I attempted to help him and the other SEALs through their business dispute, he told me about his service and his record number of kills, which I believe far outnumber the official tally (due to the DoD's onerous and unrealistic requirements for official confirmation). He asked me to help confirm this data with the DoD, which I did. Eventually, it became clear to me that Chris's life should be documented in a book. When I suggested he write one, he balked. He had no interest in drawing attention to himself.

SEALs do not fight and tell. There was an unspoken code and Chris was a private person—humble, not a braggart or self-aggrandizer. But I pressed him, believing not only that his story had historical merit, but that the public needed to understand what our warfighters were experiencing every day in two theaters of combat and at home. He finally gave in with the proviso that I help him write the book. I agreed. I even had a title: *American Sniper: The Autobiography of the Most Lethal Sniper in U.S. Military History.*

We worked together for twelve months, often in bars or in the Airstream parked outside my house, tape recorder running. Chris slowly recounted his story: his youth, his stint as a professional cowboy riding in rodeos, his life at war and all that entailed, and his struggles at home. He described these events candidly with an easy, soft West Texas voice that I knew would jump off the page if we could capture it.

The blend of a harrowing war story and a man fighting to keep his life, marriage, and sanity won the hearts and minds of readers. It resulted in an instant crossover megahit, reaching No. 1 on the *New York Times* Best Seller list in its first week and staying on that list for thirty-seven weeks. Men and women, soldiers and civilians alike—seemingly everyone wanted to read *American Sniper*. Chris Kyle was the first modern warrior celebrity.

Chris appeared on late-night talk shows, where his incongruous blend of Texas-style soft-spoken humor and humility and his outsized accomplishments made him an instant media darling, a sought-after supernova-sized celebrity war hero. The press and the people adored him. We literally had a cultural juggernaut on our hands, and it changed Chris's life immeasurably.

A little over a year after the book's publication, Chris not only possessed his own money, but he was now backed by billionaires. He had retired from the Navy, and for the first time in his life he was free to do anything he wanted—except for one significant thing. He could never live anonymously again.

I learned the impact of this one idle afternoon in February. I lay stretched out in the golden sunlight that was angling over El Capitan mountain and streaming into my living room. I could hear birds chirping in my yard and the scratching of dog paws on my porch, and I could smell the homemade goat milk soap that my girlfriend, Jodi, was making. The phone rang. I leaned over, grabbed my cell off the coffee table. A friend and former SEAL whom Chris had introduced me to was calling.

"Have you heard?" he asked matter-of-factly.

"Heard what?"

"Chris is dead."

At first I thought maybe the SEAL, who had a dark sense of humor, was joking. "Don't fuck with me like that," I said.

The silence that followed told me this was no joke.

"It's true," he said.

This did not compute. Chris Kyle had spent nearly ten years in war. He was a young man, healthy and active. For him to suddenly die back in the United States seemed preposterous. "Are you sure?"

"The information came to me directly from the highest levels—from a buddy at ST-6. Level of certainty is at 99 percent—with 100 percent being only if I was standing next to him when it happened, which I was not." He said, "Nothing is on the internet yet, as they are not certain if it was a terrorist hit, but he was shot and is dead."

My breathing increased. I rose and started pacing. "Taya, the kids?" I asked.

"Okay, looks like a single shooter, unknown motivation, family not involved."

"Is someone covering the house till motive is positive?"

"Covered highest levels." I nodded, phone at my ear. My friend then said, "Let's talk later—I thought you should know."

I learned the details of the murder shortly before they became public. Chris and his friend Chad Littlefield were shot and killed on a gun range by a troubled twenty-five-year-old Marine Corps veteran. The boy's mother had heard of Chris because of the book and media around it and asked Chris if he would try to help her son deal with his PTSD. Chris and Chad had taken the boy to the gun range as therapy.

The question I had to ask myself was clear: Did the fame that resulted from the book I convinced him to write and promote contribute to his death?

Motherfucker. I knew it had. I knew I had convinced him to court death.

Soon I'd have to look Chris's wife and young kids in the eyes knowing this. My Hell Week had begun.

As the horrible weight of the guilt I felt over Chris's death pressed down on me, I wanted to die. And I pretty much tried to make this happen by drinking alcohol, first in New York and again in Texas, leading to medical attention in both cases. Medical attention to include treatment by SEAL medics, because SEALs have a tendency to give each other "recovery IVs" after serious rounds of drinking, including B_{12} IV cocktails. The days did not get better, only worse, spiraling downward toward the day of Chris's funeral.

On a dark, cold, and wet Texas morning on the Llano Plano, friends and family assembled to put a SEAL to rest. The wind drove the rain horizontal as the motorcade left the high school parking lot of the small Dallas suburb. Another son of Texas lost, to be sent home to his Maker.

The day grew worse before it grew better, as the motorcade left the suburbs of Dallas for Austin. The funeral requiem for Chris Kyle had begun. They had shut down a major interstate freeway for nearly two hundred miles. Tens of thousands of people lined the freeway and stood in frozen salute as the motorcade went by. People wrapped in blankets in the cold driving rain, their children bundled up with them, stood on the edge of the freeway for hours, waiting to pay their respects as the funeral motorcade passed by. Men in wheelchairs displaying U.S. flags. Fire trucks on overpasses at nearly every town en route, with massive U.S. flags spread between their extended ladders. All of this went on for hundreds of miles. To say I was impressed by this outpouring of love from the great state of Texas would not be fair; I was literally blown away, and it was like nothing I had ever witnessed in my life. Actual cell phone footage of this amazing event is shown at the end of the movie *American Sniper*, which would start production in 2014.

A single word came to mind repeatedly, over and over, on that drive from Dallas to Austin: RESPECT.

The respect would continue as we laid Chris to rest in the Texas State Cemetery, the same graveyard that held most of Texas's heroes, including Stephen Austin himself. The solemn sound of over a hundred Navy SEALs pounding their tridents into the coffin of their fallen brother will never be forgotten. While we attended the reception held at the governor's mansion in Austin, Rick Perry's wife, Anita, may have said it best: "Texas has lost far more than we can replace." I thought to myself how true that really was, and that America had lost far more than it could replace.

The movie would not materialize until 2014, and Chris

would never know (while in this dimension) that it was directed by Clint Eastwood, who was our first choice from day one. Clint would not get involved in the project until long after Chris was gone, but I am confident Chris was happy when he learned of it while on overwatch.

Later that day in Austin, shattered in mind, body, and spirit, and riddled with guilt, I leaned against a polished wooden bar next to Chris's master chief. We were drinking vodka—straight and hard. News footage of the motorcade played on every TV hanging above the bar. I finally confessed to Chris's master chief, "I feel responsible for drawing Chris down a path that led to his death."

"Stop." He cut me off, intuitively knowing that look on my face. "Scott, I have placed men in positions where a second later they were shot in the head by the enemy and killed instantly. I put them right there." He took me by the chest and moved me over a foot or two to trade places with me. "I moved them right where I had been standing seconds before. I put them right into the crosshairs of a terrorist's goddamn scope." He reached out and tapped my forehead with his finger. "Tap. You are dead."

I blinked. He went on, "If that act was to stop me or my men, we could not function, individually or as a team. When it is your time, it is your time, brother." He looked at me dead in the eyes and said, "Every SEAL, from day one of Hell Week, understands this fact: Not all of us are going to make it. Period."

Those words, harsh as they were, pulled me out of the abyss I had descended into. They taught me a hard but invaluable lesson: *We all won't make it, but life goes on, you need to get over it and carry on to the best of your ability—for your sake and those you care about.*

As the COVID-19 pandemic, BLM riots, and civil unrest in our nation seem to be pulling us all into hell, I, like so many others, have been wondering: When will this be over? Will we all make it? If we don't make it, who will fail, who will die? These questions, of course, are unanswerable—we simply don't know. We will only know what it takes when we get through it and see what comes out on the other side. Given this, the only thing to do is focus on how to get to the other side—and this is the point of Hell Week.

Hell Week is the U.S. military's toughest gauntlet, a six-day period in the first phase of BUD/S, the eighteen-month training period that ends with the aspiring candidate becoming an official member of Navy Sea, Air, and Land Teams, more commonly known as SEAL Teams. Hell Week takes place approximately one month after BUD/S starts, and there are differing opinions as to why it is so early in the process. The consensus would generally be that the ultimate test takes place early in the process of making a SEAL because the Navy does not want to spend too much money on the training if the candidate is not going to make it. It is estimated that the training of a SEAL costs the U.S. taxpayer in excess of $1 million per man. Hell Week itself lasts only 144 hours, yet more aspiring SEALs will be washed out during the first three days than during the rest of all the training and selection combined. Ninety percent of those who make it through Hell Week will become SEALs. It is a gauntlet, a crucible, a test of fire. Unlike most things in our society, it has not gotten easier with time and political correctness. In fact, it has arguably gotten more difficult as this country has been at war continuously for twenty years since September 11, 2001. Many men who conduct the training have known nothing but war since they became SEALs. This brings an element of reality to those who attempt to become a member of this elite group of warriors.

The point of gauntlets has arguably been lost in a culture where "everybody gets a trophy." Yet the significance of a test proving your worth could arguably be no more important than now. From our youth, one of the toughest gauntlets for young men comes to mind: two-a-days, a football tradition meant to impress both fitness and resolve in young men attempting to "make the team." There is significance in tradition, training, and, possibly of the greatest importance, the concept of actually making that list (the Team) at the end of the gauntlet. While BUD/S training is actually an eighteen-month process to earn your trident (the pin denoting that you have become a SEAL), the most intense pain in the training is front-loaded to weed out as many candidates as possible early on. This is why Hell Week takes place generally in the fifth week of the training process. The majority of the massive amount of money needed to train the candidates through the rest of the SEAL

Qualification Training will be for after Hell Week, because approximately 50 to 70 percent of the candidates will no longer be there.

As I write these words, it is January 21, 2021, and our nation is being tested. Most of the country has been in near lockdown since April 2020. Six million Americans have tested positive for COVID-19, more than five hundred thousand have died from it, and countless others are sure to fall ill and die. And the challenges facing our nation from COVID are just a small part of the shit plaguing our nation. The country is divided by party and race, and teeters on the brink of what feels like a second civil war. The riots, and the presidential transition with twenty-five thousand troops in DC, created a reality that would barely be believed if I were writing it in a fiction novel. Life is challenging now. For most of us, 2020 sucked completely, and thus far 2021 appears to be saying "Hold my beer—you ain't seen nothing yet."

And yet the cold fact is that some of us will emerge from the year stronger, while some will give up, give in, and rely on the system to save them. Some of us have already gotten stronger. A great many have not. Many have died. Many more have given way and given in to fear and panic.

We are in the midst of a great test as a nation, our most challenging gauntlet, our metaphorical Hell Week. The nation will either learn to live, die, or beat this insidious enemy, but we cannot stop (shut down) our world, because I firmly believe that will end in certain destruction of life as we know it. The threats to our freedom may be as dangerous as the disease itself. It is my sincerest belief that the lessons in this book, the lessons of the U.S. Navy SEALs, can help us emerge on the other side—better, stronger, more united—if we can hang on, like the anonymous SEALs you will read about in the coming pages.

Hell Week is not a pointless week of torture. It is a carefully designed crucible meant to weed out those who are not physically or mentally prepared to be SEALs, to rebuild those humans who are, to make them stronger, and to create unbreakable bonds between those candidates who complete the training. Hell Week teaches those who make it that they are capable of pushing themselves far harder and further than they ever thought possible.

Some of us have wondered about ourselves: *Do I have what it takes to become a Navy SEAL—could I make it?* This book will give you insight into that. And for those interested in trying out for the SEALs, it will provide a road map and a plan to prepare yourself for this gauntlet. Should you try out for the SEALs, Godspeed. If you make it through Hell Week and the rest of BUD/S, you will emerge as one of the best warriors in the world, a member of an elite class.

Most of us, however, will never go through Navy SEAL Hell Week, nor would we ever willingly experience anything like it. I certainly never have experienced Hell Week, nor would I ever want to. And yet we *will* all experience a dark and challenging experience that will push us to our limits. We are in one of those periods now. But hell can come in any number of forms—the death of a spouse, friend, parent, or (pray not) child; med school; bullying; the loss of a job; the loss of a home; a cancer diagnosis; and so on. We will all meet hell. The goal of this book is to ensure that we are all better prepared for that idle afternoon when we are blindsided by that which we never expected.

We all can learn from these lessons of the SEALs. Be warned, however, these are not the typical soft and fuzzy pieces of self-help advice we get from most friends and our parents. They are harsh, real-world lessons, often served cold, sandy, and mean. But they work. They have helped me in what had been the hardest time in my life and will help me again in our current gauntlet. I don't wish pain and suffering on anyone. But as I mentioned at the start of this Introduction, we will all go to hell at some point. Some of us are there now. If you want to survive, learn from the SEALs. May their lessons be your guide.

AUTHOR'S NOTE

For the record, I am not a SEAL. I am a recovering lawyer and writer. I have never gone through Navy SEAL Hell Week, nor have I experienced combat firsthand. I have, however, known hundreds of SEALs, and worked closely with dozens of those brave soldiers. I count many as close friends and colleagues, and I have tried to listen and learn from them. Uniformly, Hell Week has been described to me by all the SEALs I have known as one of the most formative experiences, if not the most formative experience, in their lives. And while there is uniformity, each SEAL's experience and the lessons learned vary somewhat. Recollections of this time that have been shared with me are both big and detailed, broad and nuanced. The characters in this book are composites based on the many SEALs and aspiring SEALs I have known and worked with, and the vast majority of the events described in the following pages were described to me, time and time again, by SEALs and aspiring SEALs.

While this book is a work of nonfiction and based on facts, it is not an attempt at journalism or the simple reporting of facts. This book seeks to do something more than simply report; it seeks to present to the reader the closest possible representation of Hell Week that one can experience—to put the reader in the shoes of a SEAL at BUD/S and to let them see, smell, hear, taste, and feel what it is like to go through this crucible.

To best accomplish the goal of putting the reader into the mind and body of a SEAL leading up to and during Hell Week when referencing what a SEAL experiences—to relate that part of the narrative—I have chosen to use the second-person point of view, in which the narrative is told from the reader's perspective. In this book, "you" are the SEAL candidate. The goal of using this device is that the reader can experience, as closely as I can render, what my interview subjects have seen and experienced.

The descriptions of Hell Week you will read in this book have come directly from those who have attempted to pass the gauntlet. In some rare cases I used references from the existing and vast library of sources (books, documentaries, articles, et cetera) about Hell Week to verify, augment, or lend further insight into the experience of the SEAL candidate. Not all of the details, insights, and descriptions in the book come from SEALs. Some come from friends of SEALs, wives, girlfriends, parents, and several of the most important descriptions come from those who failed Hell Week. In all cases, I have obscured some names, identities, and events to protect my sources.

The stories of the SEALs I have either met or interviewed over the course of twenty years who have passed Hell Week are remarkably similar, but they are not entirely the same. Reflecting the diversity of our population, the backgrounds, ages, and physical and mental attributes of the men in the program vary widely. And while the training protocols in Hell Week are designed to be consistent class after class and from year to year, the training itself does change, and the nuances of each trainer and class affect the overall experience. Some of the SEALs, SEAL trainers, and commanders I interviewed for this book experienced Hell Week over thirty years ago. Some are still training as of this writing.

This book is a montage of experiences and memories taken from a vast selection of SEAL candidates over time. My work has been focused on creating a collective experience, much like a craftsman might assemble a mosaic. Any failure to accurately capture or describe Hell Week in part or in whole is entirely mine.

In my experience, SEALs are some of the most generous, honest, and outstanding individuals a country and culture can hope to produce. While I have worked with hundreds of SEALs, a select few who have helped me along this literary journey deserve mention here: Chris Kyle, with whom I wrote *American Sniper*; "Iron" Ed Hiner; Chris Sajnog; Ryan Zinke; and especially helpful to me, Ephraim Mattos. I am forever indebted to you for helping me, and readers, see what you have been through—through your eyes. My goal in writing this book is to share with our nation your strength, courage, and tenacity, when we need it most.

—Scott McEwen, January 2021, San Diego, California, USA

PART I

HELL AWAITS

CHAPTER 1

If you want to achieve greatness, you'll have to go through hell to get it. So ignore everyone, listen to your heart, and embrace the suck.

It's not easy to see out through the windshield. Your eyes try to focus, looking past the grime, the muck, and the trembling glass as your shitbox Ford Fiesta races down a dirt road toward town. The entire car, glass included, vibrates from the music you are playing as loud as the stereo will go. You're listening to old-school pump-up music, a band your uncle Nico recommended—Metallica and the song "Enter Sandman." The car stinks like stale sweat and french fries. Wafting off of some surface in the car, you can smell your girlfriend's perfume—likely from the passenger seat. She's sat there enough, talking about *your* future, laying it all out for you. "You have to come to Tech with me. Only losers don't go to college. Besides, it'll be awesome. And it's not like you're going to become Rambo or something. What do you want to do, go kill people? Why would anyone care about being in the Army? It's stupid."

Good thing she's not in the seat next to you now. Your memory of her is irritating enough. She doesn't get it. No one does. But what you know is that what you're about to do is not about her or anyone else. Lots of people have plans for you. Fuck them.

You swerve onto the highway and speed into town, where you hunt around for the strip mall where you saw the sign a few months back. You've been stalking the strip mall parking lot, trying to work up the nerve. You mean what you are about to do. You know one thing for certain—when you walk in you are committing, you are burning boats and bridges and will never turn back. Are you fucking ready?

Fuck yeah. You park a couple spots down from the Navy recruiting office, even though parking is open right in front.

You need a moment. Kill the motor. A cloud of dust wafts off your hood and blows across the lot. Your body, ears, and skin ring from the music. You're breathing hard, the August sun pounds on the Fiesta, and the temperature inside the car is already rising. It's 105 degrees, relatively mild for West Texas standards.

You check yourself in the rearview, hair okay, no zits to pop, no cuts from shaving. You came right from two-a-days where you're a third-string running back, sometimes slotback, and end zone fullback. You're the guy who rarely gets the ball. You block for the guy who does, and this pisses you off a bit, if you're honest with yourself. And it pisses you off *a lot* if you're really honest.

You're wearing your cleanest soft-collar shirt, jeans, and cowboy boots. A sopping wet T-shirt, a pair of underwear, and

shorts balled up in the backseat next to your McDonald's uniform and old sneakers are just waiting for you to put them on
after you do this. Something else catches your eye, poking out
from under the uniform—something pink and frilly. You reach
back, push aside the polyester pants, catch another whiff of
the perfume, and see a pink bra, D-cup, lying on the seat. Your
mind flashes back to Sunday after spending the morning at
church with her family and then at their house, where you told
her dad you were heading to town to meet friends for some
ice cream but instead you drove to a friend's ranch where you
knew no would find you. You wince and tuck the bra under
the passenger seat to give to her later. Goddamn, she's hot.
Will you ever see or feel a body like that again? You contem-
plate this and you honestly don't know. She's special, and what
you have together is special too. Are you ready to risk that?
Are you ready to give up going to Texas Tech with her?

Ready or not, there is something burning inside you,
maybe anger, maybe yearning to test yourself, or maybe to
prove yourself. To whom? To everyone who thinks you're a
little crazy, too short, not strong enough, a dumbass, even
though you know you're just bored. Maybe you need to prove
to your girlfriend, who says she loves you, but you know deep
down she's just testing you to see if you'll do what she wants
you to. Fuck that. Maybe you need to prove this to yourself—
you have always thought you could do more, be more, be the
one. You're smarter and tougher than anyone knows. You
should be the one who gets handed the ball when it counts.

And you know if you don't get up and go inside there and tell someone your plan, you might never do it. You need to commit. Right now. *Here we go.*

You push the car door open and the hot summer bakes you as you stride toward the recruiting office, tucking in your shirt, chirping the locks on the car behind you. You push open the office door, and the hot air gives way to cool, delicious AC. You wipe the sweat off your forehead, stride across the carpeted floor toward the recruiter seated behind a neat and ordered desk. He wears camouflage, and straightens up as you head his way. "Good day," he says, rising to his feet, extending an arm across his desk to introduce himself. "My name is Sergeant Harris. Can I help you?"

"Yes. Sir, I want to enlist," you say, and then for a moment you hesitate, you fumble with the words in your head that really matter, then feel awkward, yet you calm yourself and tell him, "And I want to join the SEALs."

The recruiter smiles in a knowing way, like he'd just heard a naïve little kid tell him, *"I want to be president one day."*

"Excellent," he says, smile widening, and adds reassuringly, "You look like SEAL material to me." For Navy recruiters, the SEAL program is the best recruitment tool of all time—it's the honeypot that lures the suckers in. Tens of thousands of kids show up at some point in their senior year of high school in recruiting offices just like the one you're in with an idea that they could be a SEAL. But when things get tough, they end up quitting and scrubbing brass or gaining a technical skill in the fleet. You don't know this at the time, but you sense it. He is holding the carrot to yank another body into the Navy. But he has no faith you'll make it.

"Please sit down," he says, motioning to a seat across from his desk. "Let's talk about what this means. And just so you know," he slips in, "but hey...if the SEALs don't work out, there's lots of great jobs in the Navy. You like computers?" Computers? This guy thinks you're a typist. You decide this recruiter is just another person you'll have to prove wrong.

"Sir, I am going to be a SEAL." You say this with a force and conviction that surprises even you. You watch his eyes as you say this. He believes you a little. He takes a moment and nods.

"Okay," he says. "Let's put a plan together."

Football season ends after the first round of playoffs, when the guy you block for gets stuffed on fourth down in the red zone when he gets spooked and tries to take the ball out wide instead of following you right up the middle. *Oh well.* Your girlfriend cries. Some of your buddies do too. Your mind has already moved on to training for BUD/S. And yet you haven't told anyone yet, only the recruiter and God. Your mom doesn't know, your friends don't know. Not even your girlfriend knows, especially not your girlfriend.

You make it a point to take action. You must move from the idea of training to actual preparation. You don't even give yourself a day off. Saturday, the day after your last loss as a senior, you wake up early and sit up in bed. Clock reads 6 a.m. This sucks. But you gotta do it. This is the start, right here.

You walk to the closet, feet sore from your final season. You pull out a pair of black combat boots. They used to belong to your uncle, back when he was in the Coast Guard. You slide your feet in and lace up the boots. You wiggle your toes. Tight. Your ankles click.

You stand. Not nearly as comfy as Nikes. But you can take it. You walk quietly through your house to the front door. You step out into the darkness of the early morning. It's cool now in Texas. The fresh air feels good in your lungs.

You move your legs, walking fast, then breaking into a light jog. You hoof it to your high school. The track is empty and the sun is just beginning to shine through the bleachers still flecked with popcorn and paper cups. You check your phone—your workout is right there for you to see. Lap one. You start to run the track at a pace a little faster than a jog. It's starting to warm up and the sweat rolls off you. You're in decent shape from football, but know that if you're going to survive Hell Week you need to be in excellent shape. You have a training regime you downloaded off a SEAL-related website. It tells you exactly what you need to do to get in shape, week by week, how many miles you need to run and how fast, how many pull-ups, push-ups, and sit-ups you need to do to not just pass the SEAL Physical Screening Test, but to thrive in BUD/S. You are going to be a beast come graduation. The real

challenge will be swimming. You're not so much of a swimmer, you're more of a sinker. If you're honest with yourself,
you'd probably be safer in the water if you wore floaties like
a little kid. And you're going to need to be able to swim 500
yards in twelve minutes to pass the SEAL Physical Screening
Test just to make it, let alone to become a proficient warrior in
the water. But you can't worry about that now. First step is just
learning how to swim, goddamn it.

To solve the swimming problem, you drive to town and
go to the city pool.

"Can I help you, sir?"

"Saw an ad in the paper," you tell the girl at the front desk.
"Y'all need lifeguards?"

You sign up to become a lifeguard just so you *have to* learn
how to swim. You give yourself no choice. The strategy works,
somewhat. Taxpayers of your town pay instructors to teach you
how to swim long distances, longer than the 500 yards needed to
pass the SEAL Physical Screening Test, and to pull a drowning kid
safely out of the deep end of an Olympic-sized pool, but you still
feel less confident in the water than on your feet, and that makes
you feel vulnerable. You tell the recruiter this, and he assures you
that as long as you can pass the PST, you'll learn "how to swim
damn good at BUD/S." Or he says, "You'll die tryin'." He's joking,
but dying is not what you're worried about. You're worried about
getting washed out of BUD/S during Hell Week.

At night when you're not dunking fries and flipping patties, you're with your girlfriend. "Do you know what dorm you're going to be in?"

"Yeah...Ugh...I got a letter." And you dodge the question.

She hasn't just planned your life for school in the fall. She talks marriage and kids. "I think I want four." And church. "We're gonna be Baptist and our kids are gonna be in Sunday school. I think I might teach...Hon, pull over here, would you?" And then you park and the aspiring Baptist tears your clothes off, pushes your seat all the way back. She cranks the radio and climbs up onto your lap, straddling you, kissing you. Country music is playing on the radio, you're on a back road, and she's working her panties off. Then she stops.

"What's wrong?"

"What do you mean?"

"You're not here. Where are you?"

"I'm here."

"No you're not. You're somewhere else—I can tell."

You run your hands up over her double Ds. "No, believe me, I'm right here."

She bats them away. "Are you cheating on me? What the fuck is going on?"

She's off you and in the other seat getting dressed. Fuck yeah, you're cheating on her—with Uncle Sam. But you say nothing, you just watch her dress in the moonlight spilling through the passenger window. You've already signed your enlistment papers—you did it after you turned eighteen. Your ass is now owned by the U.S. Navy.

"You really want me to take you home?" She sighs. She studies you. She starts undressing again.

When you're alone, you scour the internet looking for information on the SEALs. You watch a shitload of war movies—*Lone Survivor, American Sniper, Navy SEALs* with Charlie Sheen, *Black Hawk Down*—and you read books, realizing some of them had been made into the movies you love. You find an old documentary film from the Vietnam era called *Men with Green Faces*. It looks weird, like ancient history. Yet the men in it are just like you. Almost sixty years ago. You come to understand that there is one fundamental truth to becoming a SEAL—the first and last rule is do not quit. This becomes the secret mantra you tell yourself over and over every day.

You don't lie entirely to your girlfriend. You did get into Tech and you are awarded a scholarship, engineering at Tech and another at A&M. Her parents are so proud of you. Your mom cries and talks about how your dad would be proud too, if he were still here. You begin to feel guilty about your secret. One month before graduation you invite your mom, your girlfriend, her parents, and your uncle Jesse to dinner to tell them some good news. You've saved for this; you've put back on the jeans and your best shirt and cowboy boots and treat them to an early Sunday dinner at Chili's. Your girlfriend's dad wants to pay, but you insist. "What's the big news?" he asks. "You gonna be an Aggie or a Red Ranger?"

You have everyone's attention. You take a deep breath and say, "I'm enlisted in the Navy. I'm going to be a SEAL."

All mirth stops. Forks clank against dessert plates. Murmurs fill the room. Your girlfriend's jaw drops. "What?"

"Yeah. I'm gonna be a SEAL."

"You're fucking kidding me, right?" She's pissed.

After you repeat this information to your incredulous guests, both your mom and your girlfriend are crying and pissed. Her dad is questioning putting off college. "Are you sure this is the best use of your time right now?"

You tell him you have every intention of getting your degree, only later. Even your uncle, the one who'd been in the Coast Guard, tries to talk you out of it. "But you're such a good student"—which is not true, actually, you're only average—"why don't you go to school first? And the SEALs—do you know how hard it is?"

Barraged by a blur of tears and misplaced fatherly advice, you pay the check and hustle outside with your girlfriend, promising her "everything will be all right—all the dreams you had, the kids, the marriage, the house and pool one day. We'll have it all. You'll get it all in the Navy. It's a fucking great job. I'll be a SEAL."

She's standing next to you, leaning up against the Fiesta, not caring that she's getting her white jeans dusty. "But you could get killed," she says, tears running down her face, which you notice has recently been spray tanned. The tears roll off her fake eyelashes and drop into her cleavage—Jesus, she's got a helluva body. She's wearing the damn perfume too.

"It'll be fine," you tell her. "I love you, we'll make it work."

Her lashes bat heavy teardrops in the late spring air. Her big eyes roll up at you. "But I don't know if I can wait that long."

Ten minutes later you're alone, driving as fast as the shit-box Fiesta will go. You're not crying, but you're about as close to it as you've been since you were nine years old. You've just cut loose the love of your life (or maybe your ball and chain, you're still wondering), you've disappointed her parents, you basically told off your uncle, who has been your hero your entire life. And you made your poor mom cry. Nice job.

Then again, you're going to be in the Navy in a matter of weeks, and then you'll be in Coronado some months later for the real test. *Cut this shit loose*, you tell yourself. These folks love you, but they want to hold you back from your dream. You roll down the window and reach around under the passenger-side seat and pull it out. The big-ass frilly bra that still smells like the best night of your life. Fuck it. You fling it out the window.

Boot camp here we come.

Lesson:

Well-meaning others—mom, dad, family, your girl or guy—will rarely understand why you would want to give up security and accomplishment for a chance to risk everything in order to have a shot at your dreams. They will try to dissuade you from attempting a big challenge because they don't want you to get hurt. From them, it comes from a place of love and concern. Other haters will simply try to bring you down. The "safer road" is always the easier choice. This applies to climbing mountains, running marathons, attempting an Ironman, writing a book, volunteering to work with the infected, taking a medicine or vaccine that could either kill you or cure you. The risk you know you need to take, the sacrifice you want to make—these are the steps that those who love you will always try to keep you from making. Only you can make that decision, and once you decide to take on any worthwhile challenge, you will immediately be met with an overwhelming struggle.

Winston Churchill famously told the British people at the beginning of World War II as Germany set its sight on the United Kingdom, "I have nothing to offer but blood, toil, tears, and sweat." Churchill also said, "The empires of the future are the empires of the mind." I have always enjoyed that quote, because it was truly descriptive of the British Empire at that time. The "empire" that was physically controlled by the British had dwindled to the point of strategic alliances with countries that were no longer militarily controlled by Great Britain. Yet the language, teachings, law, and common heritage ("the collective mindset") of the British that were left with India, Australia, Canada, the United States, and many other former colonies allowed the tiny island to remain alive during a blitz from a continent then controlled wholly by Nazi Germany. Churchill's words have nothing to do with the Navy SEALs, but in some respects they could not be more appropriate. For those who want to join the SEALs, or take up a great adventure or a needed risk to rise above their circumstances, doing so will put them straight into a form of suffering and hell. You will be unable to control the environment you are forced to place your body into—in fact, you will be forced to endure physical challenges and suffering no sane person would ever "voluntarily" walk into. That is the first step. The next step is to realize that your mental fortitude will lay the foundation for the empire of your future.

> Here is the truth. If you want to do anything different it'll freak people out. If you want to be a SEAL, it'll scare the hell out of some people. When I decided to join the SEALs, I was still in high school and had grown up in a devoutly religious Christian sect that practiced pacifism. Initially, my decision to join the SEALs effectively cut me off from my friends, my parents, my family. I now have my family back, but to pursue this life I had to be willing to walk away from many people who I loved and cared

about. Not everyone will walk the path with you, let alone stand by while you pursue your dreams. You must pursue them anyway.

—Ephraim Mattos, former Navy SEAL
and humanitarian

If you want to achieve greatness you'll have to go through hell to get it. So ignore everyone, listen to your heart, and embrace the suck.

CHAPTER 2

If you want to survive hell, make sure you are physically prepared to the best of your ability and mentally prepared to be utterly unprepared physically.

The flight you take to boot camp is the first plane you've ever been on. You land at Chicago's O'Hare Airport and make your way to a bus that will take you to basic training at Naval Station Great Lakes, just north of Chicago. As you ride with fifteen or so other kids headed to NSGL, you reflect on your readiness. You feel damn ready. You have spent the better part of a year training to be physically prepared for BUD/S. And as the firm abs straining under your shirt can attest, the hard work has paid off. You are in rock-solid shape, and this matters. It's important for your confidence at the beach and on this very bus. You stand a better chance of realizing your dreams than the kids riding with you. If you are honest with yourself, you knew this would happen. You knew you were working harder to be in shape than 99 percent of the teenage population. After all, you will be in a special division at basic, consisting of a hundred or so SEAL candidates—a bunch of guys just like you who think they want to become the best.

What you did not expect as you stepped off the bus and onto a military base for a training regimen that is supposed to be challenging is that the eight weeks you will spend in boot camp will actually soften you. You will be weaker physically after you leave basic than before you arrived. Sure, you'll learn there's a lot of yelling in basic, a battery of tests, haircuts, a little extra PT (physical training) and SEAL training for your division, but there's also a shit-ton of knot-tying, yes-sir-ing classroom learning. It's important stuff, and you do your best to learn and to develop a reputation as someone who is committed and serious, and while it ain't exactly spring break, it ain't all that hard either. The next eight weeks will fly by and soon your abs will have a cushiony spring to them, a layer of seal fat gained by eating crappy food and reflecting the reduced workload you are putting on your body. On your own, you pushed yourself harder than the instructors at basic, and by the end of it, like a racehorse kept off the track, your lungs and legs yearn to be driven harder. When you graduate basic you feel like a proud, polite Navy student who can't wait for the next step. You feel so good and the training has been so easy that the grounded confidence you felt eight weeks ago has let you forget you're hell-bound.

The next step in your path is an eight-week Naval Special Warfare (NSW) Preparatory School in Great Lakes, Illinois, which reminds you of the summers you spent preseason training for football, and is more like the time you actually trained for the SEALs than basic. This eight-week period does not tear you down as much as you'd expected, but it sharpens you physically and mentally, getting you back into top form, and as ready as you can be for BUD/S.

And yet it's not all smooth sailing. If you struggle anywhere, it's in the pool. It's not that you're worried about failing any of the known speed and distance tests; you just don't feel as good in the water as you want to. It still feels foreign—a struggle—and sometimes underwater you become panicked. You recognize this and take extra time with your instructors and classmates to improve and become more comfortable in the water. You swim lap after lap, racking up tens of hours of extra time in the pool.

As the weeks wind down, the reality that you are getting closer to BUD/S hits you in an unsettling way. Your skin tingles with anxiety when you think about it. And as you move from one city training location to the next, one stage to the next, and one more test to the next damn test, you feel like you are part of a herd of sacred Hindu cattle, simultaneously herded, poked, prodded, and selected with the other E-1s (Grade-A meat) for a naval destiny. Every moment you have free to think your own thoughts, you try to prepare yourself mentally for what is ahead, reminding yourself over and over that no matter what, you will not quit when it gets really fucking hard. Sometimes thoughts of your girlfriend come to mind—you wonder if she misses you, if she regrets doubting you, if she still thinks about fucking you ... if she's fucking someone else, which you realize is both an unhealthy topic to have on your mind and one you can't break free of. She's got to be fucking someone. She's a smokeshow college freshman in the state of Texas, and unless she was faking it with you, she loves to have sex in cars, in barns, even in the laundry room of the Baptist church basement she spoke of attending.

On your jogs, swims, and when you work out, the thoughts sneak back into your head. You wonder who it is she's sleeping with and you begin to think of a couple guys you know well (and never really liked) who were always hanging around waiting for something to go wrong. You push the 225-pound bench in ten reps each, certain beyond any fucking doubt one of those assholes has likely snuck into her sorority house, gotten her drunk on Boone's Farm, maybe split some gummy edibles with her, and after a good hour of talking shit about you, fucked the shit out of her while Taylor Swift plays on the iPhone you gave her. You can see that dude, a guy you used to consider a bro, sneaking out of the sorority house to hang out with his friends in his dingy frat and laugh about how he just fucked your sort-of ex—while you are in a pool swimming laps in an attempt to prepare for the hardest trial of your life.

"Heyo, brother," a voice calls to you while you're on a jog. It's Klemper, a friend you have made during basic. "How's things?" He runs up in line with you.

"Alright..." You jog for a bit. "Actually, mind is kinda goin' nuts if you want to know the truth."

"Tell it, brother." Klemper is older, he's got three years of junior college under his belt, so he's more experienced in the ways of the world and the wiles of women. "And don't hold back."

You tell it. Everything you have been thinking about her as you run. "Brother, I can't stop thinking about her, man. It's killing me. I shouldn't care or think about her, but I do care. She's got to be fucking someone."

He tells you, "Dude, those thoughts are not good. Get your head right. Forget your ex-girlfriend . . ."

"Technically she's not really my ex. We didn't define a breakup, so she's pretty much my girl."

"Forget technically, technically you just told me she's balling some other dude." You wince, Klemper sees it. "I'm kidding. You don't have any idea what she's doing. She could be crying her eyes out waiting for you."

"This isn't really helping," you say.

"Know what the problem is?" he asks you.

"What?"

"If you're thinking about her, this is not hard enough for you. Trust me, we get to Hell Week, you will not be thinking about this girl. You'll be thinking about survival."

Hell Week begins to seem like relief. "I can't wait for Hell Week," you say. And you have no idea at the time how insanely naïve you are to think this.

"Yeah, man," Klemper says. "We just gotta get through this training, bro, you won't be able to fight the girls off of you once it's over, and if you ever do run into any of those backstabbers from home, they'll just be jealous you're a SEAL. And

If you let these thoughts fuck with your head now, you won't be a SEAL. You'll be scrubbing some hallway in an aircraft carrier, and when you're fuckin' doin' that, yeah, there will be a dude banging your ex."

"Fuck you," you say and laugh. But he's right. You've got to get your head on straight. *Get sharp, mentally and physically*, you tell yourself, *especially mentally.*

Following the Naval Special Warfare Prep, you are loaded onto a military plane with your class (minus the two who dropped out in Illinois) and flown to Naval Air Station North Island in Coronado, California.

Finally, your expectations of what SEAL qualification would entail begin to line up with your experience. After you land in California and climb aboard a bus on the tarmac, you are taken straight to the Naval Special Warfare Center in Coronado, where you are given new gear, a key card, and a room in a barracks. Over the next three weeks you begin to get a taste of what real PT is—you perform endless calisthenics in the famed grinder, basically a parking lot used to torture students. You begin proper SEAL swim training in earnest, and you are introduced to the "O Course," the famous SEAL obstacle course. The first time you swing your body up over the beam that holds up the net, you tense up—you're eighty feet in the air, no net, no safety harness. If you fall, you may never walk again. Depending on how you fall, if you land on your head or neck, you may never be able to wipe your ass again. You're also eighty feet above one of the most beautiful beaches in the world, as perfect waves curl along the surf and hammer the sand in the distance. This feels good but hard. Your confidence builds, and you feel like you are getting the hang of it.

When BUD/S finally begins with whistle blowing, screaming, and countless rounds of PT and beatdowns, the bell begins to ring. This is the big brass bell that hangs in the back of the grinder and follows the BUD/S class wherever it goes. To leave BUD/S or DOR (Drop on Request) all a candidate needs to do is ring the bell three times and they are given a coffee and a donut and quietly removed from the Naval Special Warfare Center.

The comfort and confidence you felt during orientation slip away as you learn what endless rounds of push-ups, sit-ups, and flutter kicks actually mean. You thought you knew. But you didn't. Now you know. Or so you think. This ain't shit, you will soon realize.

Still, it's hard because as you try to do the calisthenics, instructors spray you in the face with an ice-cold hose and scream at you. It sucks, and it's shocking how intense the instructors are, especially one trainer you begin to call the Joker. He's always smiling and laughing, but there's nothing funny about this sadistic motherfucker. Still, no matter what is yelled at you, or how sore and tired your body gets, you feel it is ready. Your intense physical preparation is paying off. You will never ring the bell. *Instructors, bring it on,* a voice calls out inside you.

At the end of day one of BUD/S you look around for your buddy Klemper. Classmates pour in and out of the locker rooms. But he's not there. He could easily have dropped. A sad feeling comes over you. He's been a good friend for the past twenty weeks or so, maybe your best friend in a while.

You head toward the chow hall, head hanging low and feeling discouraged. You move in line like a zombie for the hot trays.

"Heyo, brother..."

You spin, turning around to see your buddy Klemper, the familiar smirk on his face, but he's walking funny, with an exaggerated bowlegged stance, like he's got a bag of marbles swinging between his legs.

"'Sup?"

"You looked scared there for a second. You worried I DOR'd?"

You laugh. "Nah. How you been?"

"Goddamn, brother. It's only day one..." he says quietly, spooning a mound of chicken parm onto his plate, swinging his legs in that weird walk. "But my balls are on day sixty-fuckin-nine. I ain't had chafing like this since I tried to have sex on the beach junior year in high school." He laughs painfully. "Dude, I don't know what to do. They're all swole up, like mini cannonballs."

"Try A and D," you say. "I used that when my cup in football would cut into my legs."

"A and D your ass," he says. "I got this." He corrects

himself. "We got this, brother." He gives you a knowing look and slips past you heading for a table.

Yes. *We got this.* You believe it with all your heart.

A measly month later and your world has flipped entirely. You are on the floor of a bathroom in a motel, twisted up, spasming, body coated in a cold sweat, feverish, teeth gritted and trying to catch your breath and make it past alternating rounds of blasting diarrhea and projectile vomiting. Hell Week begins in less than twenty-four hours and you're already in hell. You're on your last weekend leave before Hell Week, and supposed to be recuperating before the "real shit" begins.

But it can't get worse—not worse than it is now. You are completely incapacitated. Still you think of your class. Nearly half of the trainees have dropped out. The group of those who are out includes Klemper, whose chafing balls were not his downfall. He did not ring the bell. He was pulled out due to VGE—viral gastroenteritis. You hoped when he was pulled out that he would get a second shot, and perhaps he will. But you couldn't give a shit about that now. You have to focus on getting yourself through.

Your balls and the insides of your legs are shredded raw, but those are the last things you give a shit about. You have much bigger problems. You're physically fucked. You have spent your precious leave lying in a motel room trying to recover from sore muscles. Instead, you probably should be in the hospital.

VGE, a rare, not widely understood infection, is common among SEAL trainees. You probably contracted it from Klemper. Symptoms include stomach cramps, fever, nausea, and near-constant diarrhea and vomiting. The infection is caused by a bacterium that lives in the water off the beaches of the Naval Special Warfare Center, and it seems to have it out for SEAL trainees. You are not the only one in the class to catch the bug, and some have left with what appears to be honor, a medical out, a golden parachute, an excuse the guys who left can tell their buddies back home. "I didn't quit. I got VGE and had to leave." Bullshit. The guys you saw leave had gas in the tank. And were not as bad as you.

VGE seems to have afflicted you particularly badly. Within a matter of about a week, all of the physical gains you had made during the eighteen months you spent preparing for BUD/S and for Hell Week have been taken away from you. You honestly did not know a human could produce so much biological waste. The toilet just inches above your head is proof to that, a trophy given to world champion double-ended disease spreaders. The porcelain bowl is flecked in enough shit and puke to re-cover the Sistine Chapel, the bathroom is a legit biohazard, the goddamn motel should call in a hazmat crew to clean it, and if you'd been back in Texas you would have begged your mother to take you to the hospital.

Contracting VGE will weaken a trainee to the point where he quits, or if he does not quit, is almost certain to require a medical deferment, in which he must recuperate and attempt BUD/S all over again, like Klemper.

That said, you also know there are plenty of SEALs who get VGE and make it through BUD/S, including Hell Week. In fact, you heard the instructor Joker tell the class, "Listen, I know a bunch of you pussies have VGE, and if you want to see a doctor and get a medical out and retake the course, that's your decision. But if you're gonna be a good dude and gonna make it to the teams, you're gonna make it whether you have VGE or not. It just sucks a little harder is all. So, embrace the suck, motherfuckers." And then he laughed.

"Fuck you, man," you say out loud, lying in your own shit and puke. And yet you wish that sadistic fuck was there with you now to help you out. You have never felt as alone as you do right now. You want to call someone—your uncle, a friend, your ex, the guy who's banging her. *Anyone.* You just want someone to help you through this. Instead, you have Joker's laugh ringing in your ears, your body won't stop shaking, and in a few short hours the sun will rise again.

Eventually you need to ruck up, get your shit together, and report back to the base to start five and a half days of physical and mental hell. *Come on,* you tell yourself. SEALs *commonly* get this disease and make it through. You realize that every serious SEAL candidate must have meticulously trained before they got to boot camp, busted their ass in NSW Prep and orientation, and all had carefully laid plans that didn't mean shit when they got the bug. What was left in them? A common determination to make it through. You commit to that. The first and last rule of the SEALs is you will not quit. You won't fucking quit. You utter a mantra, telling yourself, *The instructors may pull me out for a medical, but I will not quit. They will have to pull me out.* As you repeat this mantra, your mind calms, panic leaves, and confidence returns.

Your physical training "empire" is gone because of severe illness. Now the only thing that can carry you through the battle is your mental empire. The discipline that you have forged in your mind. Physically, shit can and will always happen. Something will break. If you have planned for it mentally, you merely shift to Plan B, and work through it until you can physically get back to Plan A.

You're going to show up in the morning and make them try to break you.

Lesson:

In life and in the SEALs, we must always prepare as diligently as possible for what we know will happen. A trainee who does not train ahead of time for BUD/S is an arrogant fool begging to lose out on fulfilling a lifelong dream. Likewise, a civilian who does not prepare for goals in his or her life is equally as foolish and arrogant. We do our homework, we study for our tests, and we rehearse our presentations, so that when we are put to the test we perform. And yet it is equally foolish and arrogant to believe we have control over fate, God, weather, or a little germ that crawled up our asses. We must also prepare for the unexpected to happen.

The good thing in preparing for the unexpected in life and in the SEALs is to have a mindset. Know what the ultimate move is that you can fall back on if all of your plans fail. In the case of the SEALs, the rule "never quit" is enough, and having a simple mantra when shit hits the fan can have a grounding effect, quiet the mind, and give you confidence that no matter what, you can complete the course. In life, the mindset needs to match the circumstance. The challenges of enduring a failing marriage are very different from those of launching a new start-up. That said, a simple mantra such as *No matter what I will be okay* or *No matter what I will not quit* will usually work when you find yourself encountering the unexpected.

The vast majority of retired SEALs I know are extremely

successful at whatever line of work they choose. Some choose to complete their education and become doctors, physicians' assistants, businessmen, you name it. A thought comes to mind of me going to Montana to attempt to help my friend Ryan Zinke become a U.S. congressman from that great state. Montana is generally known as being fairly conservative (although that has unfortunately changed some as of late due to Californication), and thus the winner of the Republican primary is oftentimes favored to win the sole congressional seat for a state the size of the entire northeastern section of this country. Ryan was running against some other former military members who had significantly more name recognition than he did. But I will tell you what they did not have—the drive of a former officer at SEAL Team Six. To state it simply, you could not outwork this individual, and I witnessed personally how he beat his competition, because that is exactly what he did. He got up earlier, drove longer, took more meetings, did more interviews, slept less, and drove his team supporting him (myself included) to do the same. If he had no time to work out, he would drop and do a hundred push-ups and sit-ups, and he would incentivize you to do the same. Not only did he win the primary, he won the general election. By the end I knew why, as not only is Ryan a great patriot and son of Montana who deserved to represent his beloved state in Congress (and ultimately be appointed to the office of secretary of the interior), but he outworked the competition. He personified the first and last rule of the SEALs: Never quit!

Preparation is everything in a team. You must have
your shit together—your kit, your A, B, and C plans,
your strength, your tactics—everything matters. It
is a sin not to prepare, because if you don't prepare
to the absolute best of your ability, you are putting
your life and, more importantly, the lives of others in
danger. That said, no amount of well-prepped gear, no
amount of workouts, no plan or backup plan is anything
compared to how you mentally prepare. The good news
is that mental preparation and your ability to calm
yourself and come up with a plan when you are down
can save you from nearly any situation, no matter how
fucked you are, how outgunned you are. Keep clear
between the ears and you'll get through anything.

—Ryan Zinke, former commander at SEAL
Team Six, U.S. congressman, and
secretary of the interior

CHAPTER 3

DAY ONE

If you want to survive hell, when it comes on, just keep crawling.

Your phone vibrates, an alarm going off. You blink awake, eyes adjusting to the light in the nondescript SoCal motel, drapes drawn, morning light flickering in. You're lying in bed, wrapped in blankets, warm, your fever mercifully gone—for now. You shut off your phone and feel a rush of energy, oddly wired despite the exhaustion and the lingering nausea and stomach cramps. It's time to check out of your motel and get your ass to base. *Move*, you tell yourself.

You shower in the befouled bathroom, dress, pack, and step out into the California sun. It's bright, but the air is brisk, and with your body still warm from the hot shower and smelling of soap, you feel clean and fresh and as ready as you can be given the circumstances. You take an Uber to base. A young guy in his midtwenties drives you, rap playing low in his Corolla with tinted-out windows and flashy rims. As you drive over the bridge to Coronado, you have a sweeping view of downtown San Diego, the harbor, and Catalina, which sits out ahead of you like a surfboard lying perpendicular to the waves in the ocean. You drive through the idyllic beach community, the bars and restaurants and fauna glimmering with Christmas lights, the occasional drunks and hipsters still staggering home from a Saturday night out. This is going to be your last real glimpse of the civilian world for nearly six days, which in reality will be more like one long day since during those days you will sleep no more than five hours. You let out a long exhale, thinking how different you will feel in just a few short hours.

You have the driver drop you off outside the base. "Right here," you say, and he pulls off by the gates to the Warfare Center.

As you get out he says, "Hey man, you a SEAL or something?"

"Not yet," you tell him. "I'm a student, four weeks into training."

"Damn, man," he says. "I hear it's really tough." He shakes his head like he's been through it all. "Hard as hell. You do that hard shit yet?"

Hard shit, you wonder. It's all hard. "You mean Hell Week?"

"That's it." He nods.

"Starts tonight."

"Fuckkkkkkkkk," he says as he squints back at you, a hard

stare coming over his face. "I hear there's a pizza place in town that gives free pizza to anyone who makes it."

"I heard that as well."

He lets out a sigh and makes a clicking sound. "Well, good luck, man." He holds a fist up. A gold bracelet hangs from his wrist. "I hope the pizza's worth it."

"Me too," you say and bump his fist.

"Semper Fi, my brother," he says. "*Semper Fi.*"

You want to tell him that's the Marines, *my brother*, but you're out of the car and on your way to take on that hard shit.

After you report in at the base, you make your way through the training compound as the rest of your hundred or so classmates hustle in from their two days of leave. It's a lot of people, but only half as many as who started, and this group is about to get even smaller. You can feel the mix of excitement and dread hanging in the air, as palpably as you can feel the mist blowing off the ocean. It touches your skin and tickles the hairs on your arms. You find your room in the barracks, unload your gear, get dressed, and head toward the grinder, that wet flat piece of concrete where your instructor will try to break you. You meet the rest of your class. After formation, and a mild beatdown, you are sent to the beach. Many of the students are clearly as sick as you, and openly vomit in front of you, as there is no other choice.

Running across the beach, in groups of twos—a "swim buddy" always near you—your class works to pre-stage the boats and logs for Hell Week. You place them along the shore.

Waves roll and pound the sand beside your feet as you scramble along dragging the heavy objects. Out in the surf, a man sits on a surfboard, chin turned to the sea, waiting for a set to come in. It's one of the instructors catching waves on a Sunday. It's winter and he's wearing a thick neoprene wetsuit. The ocean is blue, enormous and beautiful, a sight you rarely experienced growing up in Texas. This same beautiful body of water will be your biggest obstacle in the next five and a half days. The vast, cold, and sometimes violent ocean will try to kill you, either by drowning you in the waves or freezing you. And the instructors will let you ease up to the very edge of death. They will let you enter hypothermia, almost for a week straight, and then will continually drown you—literally *drown you*—to the point of near death. You must put your faith in their hands that they will lead you to the edge but keep you from slipping over. And yet, you know death happens. Hell Week can kill, has killed, and often maims those who attempt to pass the gauntlet on their way to becoming warriors. It gives you some measure of solace to know that the instructor, now riding a wave, in the relative comfort of his wetsuit, has also braved the cold unrelenting ocean and preceded you through hell. He is the gatekeeper, who demands payment before you are allowed to enter the realm of elite warriors, aka SEALs. It was difficult for him, and he will ensure it will be every bit as difficult for you. Not because he is sadistic, although some trainers may be aptly described as having this tendency, but because he knows that one day he himself may need to rely on you in battle on some distant shore, or mountain, or desert. If and when that day comes he wants no lesser man than himself watching his six.

Back in the barracks, you set aside a second clean and dry uniform in the small closet, to change into during the periodic medical checks that will occur over the next six days. Next, along with the rest of your class, you huddle in a large classroom where you will be quarantined until your SEAL instructors appear and Hell Week begins. The first unofficial training evolution of Hell Week has begun, *the wait*. The brutal wait. You know how the death row inmate feels (almost). They will go to hell and stay there. You will come out a member of the warrior elite—if you can make it. If you fail, you fail into a shame only you will know.

Sitting on the floor of the classroom, you carefully sip a bottle of red Gatorade to try and rehydrate from the morning's light work and the past week spent with your old buddy VGE. Around the room, students cluster in groups, some laughing and joking, others in careful deliberation of what awaits the class, some dissecting the rumors you all have heard about Hell Week.

A couple guys who look nervous but are trying to look tough get loud. "I don't care about PT, man," someone says. "You can PT me all motherfucking day. But I hear they are gonna piss on us. I am not down with that."

"Who gives a shit?" another classmate jokes. "They can golden shower my ass. At least we'll be warm. I'll even drink it if I have to. Bottoms up."

You zone these voices out.

Your boat crew leader, Ensign Price, comes over and squats next to you. Price is the kind of guy your mom wants to marry your little sister. He's an Ivy League–educated officer, handsome, tall, and charming in a bro sort of way. He comes from a wealthy family out on the East Coast. From what you can tell, he fell in love with the Navy because his family kept a yacht in Annapolis. He loves the brass finish on the boat, not the sweat it takes to keep the brass shiny. He's book smart and he's wallet smart. He worked in banking before going to OCS and trying out for the SEALs. You've heard him talk about his time at Goldman Sachs and the hedge funds he plans to work for after his stint in the SEALs. He's got a plan alright. Tack his trident onto his résumé and sell it. This is a lure and trap lots of SEAL wannabes fall into—fantasizing about what happens after you are a SEAL, when you rake it in. The guys you look up to talk about loving the life, "a fuckin' blue-collar-ass life," you have heard some of the most respected and badass SEALs around base say. It's work. That's it.

"Hey buddy. You ready for this?" Ensign Price grins, slapping your knee, slapping you back into his reality.

"Yeah, I'm ready to get this over with." You force a half-smile.

He looks you up and down. "You look like shit."

"I've got VGE..." You catch a look in his eye, a look you don't trust. He backs away and glances toward the door. "But don't tell the medics. I think... No, I'm getting better."

"You sure?" Price asks, his face showing genuine concern, and he leans back in his squat, distancing himself even farther.

You nod. "Yeah. I am sure."

"Damn. That's terrible," Ensign Price says, as he stands back up to put even more distance between you. VGE has ravaged your class over the past three weeks, rolling through students like death's head dominoes. As soon as one guy got it, the rest came tumbling down. He knows VGE is a death sentence for a man's dream of getting through BUD/S. He thinks your dreams are dead. He doesn't want his dreams to end as well.

"Luckily Hell Week isn't all that hard," he jokes. "Try and get some rest and feel better. We're gonna need you," he says as he walks over to a sink and washes his hands. He glances back with a nod and a smile. You can see in his eyes he's marked you a goner.

Hour after hour passes with nothing to do but wait. This is a cooling period carefully designed to make you face your doubts. Each man must mentally prepare in his own way for the upcoming battle. Without a doubt, the next six days will be a defining moment—if not *the* defining moment—in your life. Hell Week is the ultimate test of what is inside of you, what you are made of. If you make it through Hell Week, you have about a 90 percent chance of making it to a SEAL Team where you will live the life of a warrior. And if you fail to make it through Hell Week, you will almost inevitably end up being sent to the fleet Navy to live in a steel cage, polishing floors, chipping paint, and pushing a broom. Worse, you will be filled with regret knowing that you never reached your full potential.

The moment feels heavy and you take stock of what lies ahead. You want to lie to yourself, but you have no choice but to honestly assess the situation. Very likely you are doomed to fail due to your sickness.

Self-help assholes have a saying that is a total lie. The lie is "failure is not an option." This could not be further from the truth. Failure is *always* an option. Failure is a state most of us live in. We fail and make excuses because excuses are real, and failure is always there waiting for you to choose it. And in your case, failure is the likeliest option. You're not being pessimistic, but realistic, to recognize how likely it is you will fail. To not fail will be nearly impossible. Hell Week is designed to make even the strongest men fail.

The only way you will not fail, realistically, is if you hide the extent of your sickness from the instructors. You can't show any self-pity or look vulnerable, or they will pounce. You return to your mantra and recommit to giving everything you have. You will make the medics drag your limp body off the beach if they want to fail you. And if this happens and you do fail—which is a very real possibility—you have the faith that, as long as you don't quit and you show true dedication, the SEAL instructors will give you another shot with the next class. If you nearly kill yourself and the instructors stop you, you will be damn lucky to get a shot at nearly killing yourself again. *Some deal.*

As you come to assess the potential failure and decide on the only terms in which failure is an option—that is, dragged off the beach—you notice Ensign Price doing the rounds on the far side of the classroom. He passes from group to group, grinning confidently, checking in with the men, trying to rally them and keep their spirits up. But something rings false. You can't put your finger on it.

After the class wrestles with their nerves and doubts for many hours, a SEAL instructor walks into the classroom and orders everyone to file out onto the beach. "There are tents outside on the beach. Go sit in them and wait."

The last purple light of sunset can be seen far off on the western horizon as you cross the moonlit beach. You file in with the class into the dark, cramped, musty military-style tents and line up in row after row. You sit. For the first time that day, no one speaks. You smell sea air, sand, clean uniforms, and the chemical smell of fear and anxiety.

You just sit and shiver in the dark listening to the Pacific Ocean breaking, sending wave after wave crashing into the shore. Your mind recalls the chickens in your grandparents' coop at night, quietly clucking, shifting around. All those birds sat passively, awaiting slaughter.

Between the roaring sets of waves, the wind carries the hint of voices over to you. An officer who stands by the edge of the tent whispers, "Stand by." Instinctively, everyone stands in the pitch darkness and stares toward the flap of the tent. "What did he say?"

you hear. The word is passed to the back of the tent. Your heart pounds, and it's all you can hear as you stand in utter silence. There is nothing to say. Everyone knows that half of you will no longer be there in six days. Put up or shut up, motherfucker.

BAMBAMBAMBAMBAMBAMBAMBAMBAM-BAMBAM!

The deafening sound of machine-gun fire punches holes in the silence, you flinch hard, your body tenses, your heart hammers. You feel your nerves shattering. SEAL instructors outside the tents scream into megaphones, "HIT THE SURF! MOVE! NOW!"

You push through the doorway of the tent and burst out onto the beach. Blinding flashes from M60 machine guns firing blank rounds light up the beach as you sprint into pure chaos. Explosions from artillery simulators send concussive sound waves rippling through the staggered lines of students as you charge toward the frigid ocean. Without warning, your stomach spasms. You projectile vomit the red Gatorade you recently drank all over the front of your uniform. It streaks across your face as you run, in a red, crazy, gruesome smile. You do not break stride, even to puke.

You "hit the surf" and the cold shock of the ocean feels like you have fallen into an ice bath. They call you back and you stagger out of the waves, soaked, legs waking back to life, and sprint back to the instructors.

"HIT THE FUCKING DECK! CRAWL! DON'T FUCKING LOOK AT ME!" an instructor screams into the megaphone.

The class drops to the ground and begins to crawl through the soft sand. The machine-gun and artillery simulators act like camera flashes on the boots of the man in front of you. As he crawls frantically toward the BUD/S compound, his feet occasionally kick you in the face and crush your hands. You do the same damage to the poor soul crawling behind you. But the man behind you has a surprise coming. Again, you cannot help it—you puke onto the sand in front of your face and then crawl through it. He doesn't even notice and crawls right through your diseased VGE puke like a worm. Sorry, dude.

The BUD/S compound had been converted into an urban war zone. Heavy weapons and small-arms fire crackles overhead as you continue to scurry flat on your stomach through the empty parking lot. Instructors with fire hoses spray you with freezing water and order you to do push-ups and flutter kicks. Your knees and elbows start to blister and bleed from crawling around the concrete compound.

Amid this chaos, you become dimly aware of a pungent chemical odor you have never smelled before. You peer up to see a cloud of green smoke rolling toward you like a giant snake, its pale belly lit up by the explosions and gunfire. The cloud of smoke smacks into you, and you attempt to bury your nose and face into your shoulder. But you inadvertently breathe some in, and the oxygen is squeezed out of your lungs. Like a snake wrapping around your neck, the gas seems to wrap around your body, causing your muscles to tense spasmodically, and it feels like something is crushing your rib cage. You can't breathe, your vision blurs, and tears involuntarily run down your cheeks. You cough violently and manage to suck in more of the green smoke between the outbursts of vomit that now purge from you repeatedly, without end.

A sudden blast of freezing water slaps against your face. It makes you look up. A SEAL instructor stands over you blanketed by the dissipating smoke, screaming down at you. "What the hell is the matter with you!? You clearly can't keep up! Just quit right now and end this!"

You ignore the instructor and crawl through your vomit to follow the feet of the man in front of you. You shoot a quick glance behind you and see that somehow you actually are the last man. For a brief moment, you are confused and terrified—did the entire rest of the class quit? Are you in the right spot? You wonder this until you realize the instructors had ordered all the men behind you to crawl in different directions, therefore suddenly making you the last man. Now you panic, as this is the last position you want to be in. It means you will be perceived as slacking and will become a target for attention. The instructors pounce. You ignore them and fight to keep moving.

The chaos of the night—the machine-gun fire, explosions, smoke grenades, crawling, vomiting, fire hoses, and push-ups—continues for hours, until it feels like background noise. You are almost used to it, and feeling relaxed again, when the gunfire abruptly stops. There is a long period of quiet. You realize you have survived the training evolution. What's next? You don't know. But it occurs to you—you have survived the start of Hell Week.

Lesson:

We have all heard the expression "shock and awe." It is a tactic often employed by militaries where through the use of overwhelming force the enemy is surprised, demoralized, and loses the will to fight. The enemy literally is filled with shock and awe by the display of might and power.

This principle does not apply only to the military. Shock and awe is used in sports. Think of what happens in a football game when a team comes out on fire and quickly takes a 14-point lead: The opponent often gives up and the game is over before it gets going. The principle of shock and awe is used in business, in negotiation, in family and social interactions. Lawyers often try to use shock and awe in their cases—trust me, I have.

The effects of shock can also be seen in how most of us react to natural disasters and acts of God. Just search the internet for "tornado aftermath stories" and you can see it in the faces of men and women looking at their obliterated homes. Disease—especially viral disease—seems to act the same way. Right now, much of the world is in a state of paralysis caused by shock and awe, as if the coronavirus has caught us with a vicious uppercut.

Hell Week too begins with carefully choreographed shock and awe. The intent is to freak those out who are likely to quit, to overwhelm the students and make them believe they cannot possibly survive the rest of Hell Week, if it is like this first day and night. While it is certainly startling and awful, the truth about the tactic of shock and awe is that the effects wear off rather quickly. If you don't quit, the shocking violence of action with the start of Hell Week rings hollow after a while. You get used to it.

In World War II, Britain was nearest to capitulation in the first few days of bombing. The "Blitz," aka blitzkrieg, which is German for "lightning war," was on. For fifty-seven nights London was bombed mercilessly. After the shock and awe wore off and the English people dug in and showed their grit, it was Adolf Hitler who was shocked that the English were not giving in so easily. The football team that keeps its head on straight, even after a huge deficit, can come back. The family that loses their home after the tornado or hurricane can find new shelter—ideally on safer ground. There is a point when lawyers shouting becomes merely hot air, and there is a point when we figure how to live with a pandemic.

To survive this initial onslaught, the best way forward is often to just stay calm and keep crawling, even if it means you must crawl through puddles of your own puke.

When the guns start popping off in battle most people freeze up. It is a natural reaction to such extreme stress. When people get knocked down after being wounded, that's when they go into shock. When the untrained warrior realizes he is shot, and you let the shock take over, that is when he begins to die. When things go bad and overwhelm us—that is when we tend to stop. What Hell Week taught us as SEALs is to keep moving, no matter what. You can always inch forward, you can always make progress even if you are pulling yourself forward with your teeth. Never ever stop. When I was shot in the leg during a battle in Mosul, Iraq, the initial shock to my mind and my body was substantial. Then, after almost being run over by a tank assisting us in the operation, I instinctively went into my SEAL training mode; the round that had gone through my leg had not hit bone or a major artery. I was still able to put some weight on the leg. There was no QRF [Quick Reaction Force] in this battlefield, and the enemy rounds were still pouring in relentlessly. I literally had to get myself, and my team of fellow warriors, off the battlefield, or we were done. My SEAL training took over, and I repeated to myself to get through the pain and the confusion, "I am a fucking Navy SEAL, I am a fucking Navy SEAL." It worked. I reengaged and got back into the fight for both my life and that of those we were trying to save in Mosul from ISIS. The SEAL instructors were not standing over me screaming "RING THE BELL," but they may as well have been, because I realized why they had the bell. When you are in battle, "the bell" (quitting) cannot exist as an option...period.

—Ephraim Mattos, former Navy SEAL, author of *City of Death*

PART II

THINGS GET REALLY FUCKING HORRIBLE REALLY FAST

CHAPTER 4

DAY ONE (LATER)

If you want to survive hell, first win the battle in your
mind and your body will follow.

I t's like someone yanked the cord out of a giant stereo. The
cacophony of war is replaced by the distant and gentle sound
of rolling waves crushing sand—like what you'd play for a
baby to fall asleep. Mood music. We are in Hell Week and the
hardest thing to do right now is not just relax and drift off
to sleep. Then the singular voice of a SEAL instructor cuts
through the serenity. He speaks calmly into the megaphone.

"Ladies, please crawl on your faces to the obstacle course
for Log PT, if you don't mind." You recognize the instructor's voice. It is the Joker. Joker... The instructor's face is
even scarred. He has a long cut down his left cheek. It almost
looks like a film makeup artist painted it on to make him look
evil and dangerous. Rumor, funny enough, is that the scar is
not from a bullet or a knife or something badass but is there

because he had a big-ass mole removed as a kid. Which actually makes sense. This asshole was tortured as a kid for having a huge hairy mole on his face. Girls would laugh at him, guys would tease him and kick his ass until he learned to kick ass back. His anger and sadism carried him through the SEAL training, and now he gets his revenge on the world, on us. He gets paid to tear people apart. Nice work if you can get it.

He smiles at your pain with pleasure, in a much too genuine way. Most instructors dish out beatdowns because they have to weed out the men who will quit under incredible stress from those who won't. Joker likes the beatdowns. He gets off on it.

You crawl back to the beach as Joker works the mic. "Also, just a public service announcement, this is going to hurt. Very, very fucking badly. A few of your classmates have come to their senses and are about to head in for a hot shower and a night of sleep. Why don't you join them?"

You ignore him and continue crawling through the soft sand. Small grains of sand work their way into the open cuts on your knees and elbows.

"No? No takers!? You're just going to ignore me!? Roger that! We tried to be reasonable with you, but now YOU'RE ALL FUCKED!" He screams and sets down the mic, takes a few steps toward the nearest student, and with a swing of his leg punts a square foot of sand into the man's face. The student tries to blink the sand out of his eyes and sways as he crawls, coughing and choking. "FUCKED!" Joker yells. And with that, the entire cadre of SEAL instructors descends like hyenas, shouting insults and kicking sand into the faces of crawling men.

"You think it's okay to just ignore us!?"

"Oh, you fucked up now!"

"You want to do this the hard way, huh!?"

Eventually, you reach the obstacle course, where a series of telephone poles lies waiting for your group. "Formation!" an instructor yells. You form up into teams of seven men and you stand next to the logs, ready to begin Log PT.

Log PT is a training evolution in which teams carry telephone poles and perform different exercises and races. The purpose is not only to learn how to work as a team, but also to identify those who are not willing to carry their share of the weight. If each man does his part, it's not so bad, but if one or two men slack off, the rest of the team is crushed from bearing the extra weight.

"Up log!" an instructor yells before anyone is ready. You and your team lift the log to the chest position. And then it happens once more—you puke all over yourself and the log.

The other members of your boat crew turn and gape in disgust and disbelief. "Dude, what the hell!?"

"Don't worry." You try to breathe. "I'll stay in this position. No one else has to touch this shit but me."

"Shut up! Extended arm!" the instructor screams.

In unison, your team shifts the log to their right shoulders, and then lifts it above their heads as high as they can. Your hands struggle to remain in control of the log as it is slippery and coated in your slimy bile.

Headlights sweep over the beach and a truck pulls up. Hitched to the back is the bell from the grinder. The bell will be with you every minute of Hell Week, a temptation. All you need to do is ring it three times and your suffering is over—for now. Students who quit BUD/S are put on suicide watch. This is because after they get warm and a belly full of food, the real suffering begins—one moment of weakness followed by looking ahead at a lifetime of regret.

The passenger-side door to the truck opens and Joker saunters out. "Ladies, we gave you the opportunity to quit, but you refused. So now we're going to stay out here all night until every single one of you quits. Don't blame me. You did this to yourselves. You made me do it to you." He mocks your class.

Your entire team grunts from pain and exertion as your arms begin to shake from the crushing weight of the log.

Ding! Ding! Ding! The ringing of the bell cuts through the grunting and groaning as another man quits, hiding his face, which is filled with tears.

"YES! YES! Music to my ears!" Joker laughs into the megaphone. "It's working, boys. The pussies are leaving. Go ring that bell and cry yourself to sleep."

The boat crew next to yours suddenly lets out an "aaahhhhh" as their strength fails and their log drops to the ground.

"Get that log back up!" Instructors swarm the men screaming insults and threats.

One by one, the teams begin to falter and break—including your crew.

"Okay, roger that! We tried to be nice, but you don't want to listen to our instructions!" Joker sets down the megaphone and starts walking out onto the beach. "Here's what we're gonna do. Seeing as how your weak, pathetic arms are tired, how about we go for a little walk? Follow me!"

Joker begins walking away from the class into the darkness toward a soft sand road that follows the coast and has been aptly nicknamed "the Trail of Tears." Each boat crew desperately picks up their logs and races after Joker. The teams in the back of the procession will be punished for "lack of work ethic."

For the next two hours, the instructor leads the teams over sand dunes and across the beach into the ocean, back over the sand dunes, and back down the Trail of Tears. Students start dropping out with increasing regularity, each man preferring to ring the bell rather than take another step carrying a log through the dark night and soft sand. Meanwhile, you continue to vomit on the log until your stomach runs out of fluids, and you start to dry-heave. Exhausted and shaking from both the muscle fatigue and the unforgiving cold, the class finally returns to the starting area where you first picked up the logs.

"Extended arm!" Joker says over the megaphone.

With shaking limbs, you and your team lift the telephone pole over your heads and raise it as high as you can.

"Forty-five seconds," Joker says. "All you have to do is keep the log up for forty-five seconds. Really, though, how am I supposed to trust you to cover my back in combat if you can't follow simple instructions and hold up a log? Just forty-five seconds," Joker says wistfully. And time ticks by. It's a long forty-five seconds. In fact, you are sure it has gone way past forty-five seconds. Joker repeats, "Just a little bit longer and you'll have my trust, you fucking bitch."

Muscles failing, you lock your knees, elbows, and lower back in an attempt to buy yourself just a few more seconds.

Involuntary gasps of painful desperation can be heard as all the boat crews—including yours—near the point of complete muscle failure while fighting to keep the log above their heads, which will be an impossible task at some point. And Joker wants to find that point.

"Come on, guys, hang in there!" a member of your boat crew shouts, trying to encourage your team.

"Shut up! Shut the fuck up!" Joker screams at him. "Nobody wants to hear your helpful bullshit, Dr. Phil!"

Without warning, Ensign Price, the Ivy League crew leader who is one man in front of you, lets go of the end of the log and drops to the ground.

You are not prepared for the sudden extra weight now on you. You feel a pop in your lower back, followed immediately by stabbing pain. "Down log!" you scream, nearly dropping the log.

The other members of the boat crew feel the sudden transfer of extra weight and know instinctively what happened.

The log wobbles and the team can't control it anymore.

Along with the log and the rest of the team, you drop onto the sand.

Oddly, the instructors do not swarm on your group right away. They're completely focused on Ensign Price, who still lies on the sand. He's on his hands and knees making a retching, grunting sound, gasping, like he's puking but nothing is coming up. You hear him whimper while he gasps, "Sorry... It's VGE...Give me a second."

VGE, are you kidding me?! you want to shout. *He's faking it!* This officer, this leader who would not go near you just a few hours ago, is pretending to be sick. You are shocked and disgusted. And you don't need to say anything. Everybody knows.

Your class proctor approaches Ensign Price. "There is nothing wrong with you, *sir.*" He says this matter-of-factly, adding derision and scorn with the word *sir.* "You are a coward and a disgrace, *sir.* You just abandoned your team, *sir.* You are failing at leading, *sir.*"

Joker notices the rest of us standing idly and gawking in disbelief at the officer. "What are you looking at? Get that log up!" He rushes at you, kicking sand.

Bending over to pick up the log, you realize you can no longer bend at the waist—your lumbar spine has seized up. Stabbing, violent pain courses through your spine as you drop to your knees and get under the log with a straight back in order to help the team lift it up. Not only are you sick, but now you have a spinal injury just a few hours into Hell Week. You are doomed.

You force back tears from the pain in your spine and, with the rest of the team, lift the log back over your head. Because Ensign Price is still lying in the sand getting berated by the SEAL instructors, including Joker, who is actively punting sand in his face, your team now has one less member to carry the log.

"Do you need to see the corpsman?" a neutral, quiet voice says in your ear. Corpsmen are the enlisted medical specialists who attend BUD/S, constantly evaluating trainees.

Confused, you turn your head to see the class proctor standing about a foot away from you looking you up and down. Seeing the confusion on your face, he points to your back. "Do you need to see a corpsman?" He repeats the question: *"Do you want to see a medic?"*

You can't tell if he is messing with you, but after a moment of silence, you realize he is dead serious. You feel a rush of panic. *He knows.* He knows you are injured. You are exposed. In BUD/S, SEAL instructors notoriously target the vulnerable. They identify the mentally and physically weak and harass them relentlessly, like a pack of wolves who prey on the slowest animals in a herd. The instructors smell fear and weakness and feed on it. You think back to the beginning of the day and the simple decision you made. *Make him drag you off the beach,* you tell yourself. *Do not let him trick you into admitting you are hurt.*

"No sir," you say, shaking your head and looking away from him.

He waits for a long pause, watching you, then says, "Good." Out of the corner of your eye, you catch a quick nod of approval and a glance at your name tag. He then turns and walks away, toward another struggling boat crew.

Ensign Price is still lying in the sand, dry heaving. Despite his Ivy League diploma, naval officer status, and all his talk of Goldman Sachs and hedge funds, and despite being healthy and physically fit, Ensign Price is probably going to fail less than twenty-four hours into his Hell Week. It looks like Joker is actually going to kick him in the face. If he did, your boat crew would be happy. They view Price as a traitor. The guy is a dick and *maybe he is sick*, you tell yourself. If he is sick, like you, he will need all the help he can get. The first thing he needs, however, is to believe he can make it. You suddenly find yourself speaking to him. You are actually yelling. "Price! Do not give up! Make them drag you off! Ensign Price!" He looks up. "Make them drag you off. Don't quit. Don't fucking quit!"

Price stares at you, lost, like a man who is nearly asleep looking out from a bedroom window. Then you tell him, "Wake up, man! You don't need to quit. You got this. Step up!"

Joker peels himself away from Price and comes running your way. "What the fuck did you say? He's a coward and you want to encourage him? You dipshit. You want me to put your ass down, motherfucker?" Joker is screaming in your face, spit flying. You need glasses and a raincoat. You can smell pastrami and Certs on the fucker's breath. "You mind your own business, or I'll make you my special project."

"Yes sir," you say, and you see behind Joker that Ensign Price has risen very wobbly to his feet. But he gets under the log, and you hear him mutter "Step up" to himself. You feel the shift. He lifts the log. *Fuck yeah.* He's back.

He glances over his shoulder to you and nods. He looks like a new man and yet nothing changed. He just decided to become harder, harder to bend, harder to break, harder to kill. Log PT continues on endlessly, until the first rays of light peek over the horizon. Looks like the both of you may just see morning.

Lesson:

Mindset is everything. Mindset *is* everything. Your mindset determines how you interpret the world, your senses, your existence. When you feel pain, extreme pain, you can choose to succumb to it, ignore it, or even thrive off it. Your mindset is entirely under your control, in fact it is the *only* thing you can control. This is true in life as it is in the SEALs.

You made it through day one of Hell Week because you had won the mental battle before the first shots of Hell Week were fired. You mentally were ready and your body—fucked up as it was—had no choice but to follow. And Price's did too. You both made it thanks to what was in your head.

We can win or lose before the trial begins. Having the courage to face our fears requires acknowledging weakness and having a plan to rise above it. Most people are defeated before the battle begins, primarily because they do not honestly take stock of their fears and weaknesses. They have no plan and believe that because they have won most of their lives before a true test, they will win again. What they don't realize is that they have spent their lives relying on luck and environment—birth, schools, connections—to carry them through. They expect to win and have committed a grave blunder of ego.

Ignoring the reality of our challenges and pretending they will not be hard or that we can easily surmount a real challenge is dangerous and foolish. Not realistically assessing risk is how you get your ass kicked early in a fight, how you lose a court case, or how the likeliest of candidates almost quits less than twenty-four hours into the six-day challenge.

We often think we can get by with bravado, but in a true test it will always fail if all we have is our oversized ego, misplaced confidence, and energy. We must avoid this mistake by assessing our weaknesses and limitations and figuring out how we will get through to victory. Taking the first step toward this can seem daunting. And most of us do not engage in activities where our plan to make it through a day is "let them drag me out of here." But the lesson is the same. No matter what your challenge is, know where you are weak and plan for victory. When you have a plan to follow, you know what to do when shit goes haywire, you know—literally—where to place your next step. When you know what to do in the worst-case circumstance, you can then take that step and your body follows! Have the courage to begin, to face failure, to knowingly throw yourself into what amounts to torture. When you knowingly do this, it only follows that you will come out victorious.

As a Navy SEAL officer one of my jobs was that I led phase one of BUD/S for five years. I get asked all the time what determines whether a candidate makes it all the way through BUD/S to become a SEAL—is it their training, their physicality, their smarts, their innate athleticism? After seeing thousands and thousands of men try and the few make it, I can say without question, the greatest factor is that the SEALs that make it simply decide to make it. They make a choice. No matter what, I will make it. And they never back off. This is the SEAL mindset. It can be made at any point in BUD/S. The best make it before they arrive. Some make it midway through. It doesn't matter. All make it. And once the decision is made, it is forged in steel.

—Lieutenant Commander "Iron" Ed Hiner, former Navy
SEAL and training officer at BUD/S

If you want to survive hell, first win the battle in your mind and your body will follow.

CHAPTER 5

DAY TWO

If you want to survive hell, learn to let go but never quit.

Your eyes burn from saltwater, wave after wave of freezing, sandy ocean water rolling over you, shooting up your nose and filling your ears. You have been lying flat in shallow water off the beach for an hour. You feel like an old torn, limp rag that has been dropped into a washing machine set to a cold cycle. Your brain sloshes back and forth as waves try to beat apart every fiber of your clothes, your body, your being.

"Height line!" the SEAL instructor yells into the megaphone. You try to stand and nearly fall over from the vertigo induced by the waves pounding on your head and the water in your eyes and nose. You stagger and struggle to rise up out of the punishing sea and stand and walk to safety, even though you are trying desperately to obey the instructions and get out of the fucking freezing water. The height line offers momentary reprieve from the freezing water, if you can get in line first, but you can't move. Shut off from normal blood flow due to the hourlong exposure to extreme cold, your arms and legs feel like lead weights and your hands shake violently from the mild hypothermia that has overtaken your body.

"I said height line!" the instructor shouts again. You strain, and up you go. You take a few steps and are knocked down by small waves. Your feet just gave out. But you're moving now.

And so are eighty or so remaining students as they repeat "Height line" and begin to limp in a bone-cracking zombie-like transition, as you and your classmates plod from the waves to the sand where you form one single line. A height line is what it sounds like. It's the kind you'd see on a kindergarten playground, a bunch of people formed from shortest man on one end to tallest on the other.

The beach now lies in shadow. Brilliant hues of the fire-colored sunset of orange and hazy purple dance along the surface of the ocean as the sun inches its way closer and closer to the western horizon, where it will remain hidden until the next morning. *Don't even think that far ahead,* you tell yourself. Having successfully completed the height line, the group stands shoulder-to-shoulder facing the darkening ocean, waiting for the next order as the cool ocean breeze stings your faces and an instructor counts off by groups of seven, starting from the shortest man and working his way to the tallest. The point of the height line and this method of grouping is to form groups of roughly evenly divided heights. The exercise awaiting is one of the simplest, most mundane, and yet most challenging in all of military training. You will be carrying boats in groups of seven, and by making the groups roughly the same height, the instructors are ensuring that we will all suffer the boat's weight evenly.

With dark blue lips and row after row of chattering teeth, the entire class shakes uncontrollably. You and your fellow men hunch over slightly, cramped arms folded across your chests for warmth, fingers curled around each arm. The evening breeze kicks up, adding more cold to the unbearable misery imposed by the cold, unrelenting, and unforgiving ocean.

One instructor apparently thinks everyone looks too comfortable. "Hands up!" he shouts, demonstrating what he wants you and your group to do.

You raise your bent arms above your head as best you can. Opening the body up like a sail ensures that any semblance of body heat quickly dissipates into the air blowing across your chest and cutting through your soaked uniform.

"Ahhhh, much better." The SEAL instructor laughs.

It is Monday afternoon of Hell Week. You and the remaining students in the class are less than twenty-four hours into the ungodly trial and the instructors show no signs of letting up. In fact, things only seem to get worse as time goes on. With each passing hour, the sand that covers literally every inch of your body abrades deeper and deeper into your skin, which has been softened from being soaked every minute of the day. Your skin is like a flimsy wet sponge and every single step taken tears the sponge a little more, worsening the bloody chafing between your legs, under your armpits, and along your beltline, as rough sand rubs away your flesh. Klemper's balls had it easy compared to this shit.

"Good evening, gentlemen. And a fine Southern California evening it is indeed." You recognize a familiar voice over the megaphone. You see that sadistic motherfucker Joker grinning, megaphone in hand. The victory you felt you had last night fades. The afternoon shift of SEAL instructors has switched out and the night shift has come on, signaling the beginning of what you know will be nothing short of a cold version of Dante's *Inferno*. "You'd better fucking respond to me when I talk to you!" Joker snaps.

"Good evening," the group says weakly through chattering teeth, hands still in the air, bodies losing much-needed heat.

"You all seem *so* cold," he says with a shiver and mock concern in his voice. "Well, I promise you, gentlemen, *this* isn't cold—you'll experience true cold in just a little bit. That I assure you. I want you to know this fact. One fact alone should be in your mind when you think of our time the next few hours here." Joker paces, a proud peacock. "I am promising you one thing—misery. Fucking misery. I am going to make you fucking mmmmmmiiiiiiissssssssserrrrrraaaaablllle." He waits, moves his eyes down the height line, like he's watching his voice carry on the wind and then cut through us. "Do you understand me?"

"Hurrah, Instructor!"

"Good, because I want to give you a chance." He steps across the beach. Your mind goes to Nazis, goose-steppers. This fucking piece of shit wants to terrify you, you think to yourself as he says, "One little itty-bitty chance to avoid a whole lot of fucking pain. Who is ready? Who wants to fucking quit? The bell is right there."

He points to a pickup. The bell hangs off the back, shining red in the ambient glow of brake lights. "Your salvation is right over there. Go fucking ring that bell. Someone go ring that bell!"

He looks up and down the line. "Last fucking chance." No one leaves. He shakes his head solemnly. "Fuck it, then. Time to beat you down. Now, I know all you ladies like to watch the sunset, drink your wine, relax. Maybe watch a Netflix show. That's what some dude is doing right now, in your home with your girl." He walks slowly back and forth in front of the height line. You shiver, yet you feel warm, you're getting pissed. "Why don't we enjoy a little mood music together? One of my favorites, as you watch the night snuff out any hope of you not sucking so bad as long as I have you with me."

Joker walks to the back of the pickup, where there is a speaker. As he extends the megaphone toward the speaker there is an earsplitting moment of feedback, then when Joker gets the megaphone into position to amplify the sound from the speaker we hear a hiss. Then familiar guitar chords play ominously before two voices sing the words we know so well.

"Hello darkness, my old friend..."

The Simon and Garfunkel song "The Sound of Silence" plays from the back of a pickup truck, with a group of SEALs hovering like jackals.

"You ladies look a little too relaxed. Why don't you watch the sunset from the leaning rest position?" Joker says, a smirk on his face. Then he says with a long roll of the tongue, "Drrrrrrrrrooooooooooooppppppppppp." *Leaning rest* is a military euphemism for push-up position. You quickly drop, and, arms feeling like they do not belong to you, assume a push-up position. "And look at the sunset. Take it in, girls."

It is next to impossible to keep your body in a stable push-up position in the soft sand while also raising your head to look at the horizon. Your feet and arms slowly slip and your back sags until you readjust your hands.

"Say goodbye to the sun, gentlemen," Joker says, walking along the line, his feet practically doing a soft-shoe on the sand, loving the moment. "You have no idea how beyond fucked you are. Many of you will quit before the sun rises tomorrow morning. Do yourself a favor and end it now."

"When my eyes were stabbed by the flash of a neon light that split the night..."

Out of the corner of your eye you see a body running, head down, to the truck.

Ding! Ding! Ding! The bell rings. A student has suddenly realized he no longer wants to do what it takes to become a Navy SEAL. You turn away before you can see his face. You'd have to strain to keep looking to see who quit. That would use up effort and energy better spent elsewhere. And honestly, you don't care. *Bye-bye, motherfucker. This isn't for you.*

The last few rays of the sun are swallowed by the black ocean as the bell continues to ring. "The Sound of Silence" is literally and figuratively cut short.

"On your boats!" comes the order. "Rig for land portage."

Running in a tight cluster with the seven men of your boat crew, you hustle to the inflatable rubber boats lying in a neat row on the sand right where the last group left them. When you get to the boat, you look around at the other members of the crew and realize there are only six of you. Your gut twists. You feel sick, like you have been punched in the stomach. The difference one man can make, even in a group of seven, is substantial. A seventh set of hands can be the difference that carries you through the evolution. "Where the hell is our last guy?" you say as you spit sand and swivel your head around, looking for a dude running up to you from behind. No one to be seen. You know this, yet you look anyway.

"He quit," says Ensign Price, who again is your boat leader, by virtue of rank alone. He has lost all presence that would grant him a leadership role in nature. His hollow eyes look wearily at the sea, jaw clenched yet muscles trembling, all the fight in him nearly wrung out. All of the bluster wrung out long ago. "We're fucked," he says, shoulders dropping. He shakes his head, which is hanging from his white limp neck. "We're down too many men to do a land portage."

Land portage is a team event consisting of long-distance runs and drag-race sprints all while carrying a boat on your head. It may sound harmless and odd, but it is one of the single most effective ways to break down even the strongest men and to slowly and methodically weed out the weak and uncommitted. "What are we going to do?" Price mutters to no one.

"Keep moving," you hear yourself say to yourself, but it comes out loud. The men look to you. "Just keep moving." They nod.

"How do you know?" a man asks.

You shrug. "What choice is there?"

You have seen so damn many books, movies, and television shows highlighting SEAL training, you thought you knew it all. Certainly, you knew every kind of exercise you'd encounter in Hell Week long before you got here and tried to gauge the difficulty. It was easy to understand what the difficulty of Log PT would be, same with surf torture and soft-sand runs, because before arriving for BUD/S you had lifted heavy objects (you'd even trained trying to carry logs). You'd experienced the ball-chilling shock of cold jumping into an ice-cold lake (and jumping out), and you'd gone on enough beach jogs before to know how much it sucks. But before BUD/S you'd never carried fifty pounds of weight directly on the top of your head and had to run for miles at a time, with the motherfucker instructor perched up there. It is one of the most brutal parts of BUD/S that no one, including you, is prepared for when they arrive. But boy, do you know how much it sucks now.

"Fuccckkkkkkk . . ." the man says.

"Yeahhh," another says.

"This is gonna be fun," says yet another. And you all laugh. Then the feeling among you tightens.

All the remaining men on the boat team shoot knowing glances at each other as they secure life jackets, helmets, and paddles inside the boat. With one less man, the team will not only have to carry the extra weight, but the group will likely be slower than the other crews, which means falling even farther behind, which means more beatings and a vicious cycle of suckage.

"Hurry up!" an instructor shouts as he walks by, then asks, "Where's your seventh man?"

Ensign Price straightens and, collecting himself, says, "Our seventh man quit, Instructor."

The SEAL smiles, shakes his head, and says, "I fucking love it. Ha!" He abruptly walks away, laughing, shaking his head, like he'd just swaggered out of a comedy show.

"Up boat!" The order comes from the Joker, holding the megaphone.

Your crew of six men raise the boat. Together, you set it on your heads. The sand from the bottom of the boat digs into your already bruised and blistering scalp, and its weight compresses the disks in your neck. The key to carrying a boat on your head is not to passively let it push you down, but rather to actively push up and against it with the top of your head. The pain is excruciating, and the method is unnatural to say the least, but it's the only way to carry your share of the weight.

The groans and shouts of crews adjusting their boats on their heads echo through the now dark night. SEAL instructors pull out flashlights and headlamps to shine in your eyes. The sudden sound of diesel pickup truck engines rumbling above the rhythmic roar of breaking waves confirms what all already knew is about to happen. A journey is about to begin, alright. Truck engines mean you will not just be traveling, but you will be traveling *far*. Directly behind your class is a rugged off-road ambulance. The ambulance will stay close. The class will need it. Following along behind it is a small fleet of pickup trucks carrying everything from emergency water to extra gear to boats and the bell. Always the bell. The option to fail will be ever present. It is a tempting choice that many will select in the coming hours.

Before anyone is ready, a pickup truck starts driving south, tires slipping in the sand, exhaust pouring out the tailpipe, the truck speeding away from your boat crew.

"Catch up!" the instructors scream.

Knowing that the slowest crews will be punished, a mad dash ensues as teams race after the truck with boats on their heads, fighting to be the first in line, rushing into the cloud of exhaust. Inflatable boats bump into each other in a twisted game of bumper cars. Some students scream at other crews to get out of the way, while others scream at weak members of their own crew already beginning to falter.

Your group pushes into the middle of the pack and starts running after the truck. The sandy bottom of the boat bounces on top of all of your heads, creating a nearly indescribable feeling of exquisite misery. It's a painful mix of stinging, grinding, and compression that starts at the scalp and shoots down along the spine in bright bursts, like heat lightning radiating down your nerves. The tendrils of flashing pain crackle all the way from your crown to your fucking toes. Your toenails feel like they are sparking. By now, the muscles in the injured area of your back have hardened and balled up, like rocks around your lower spine. The freezing water of the Pacific in this moment is now your friend. The ice-cold water that had rushed around you for the past hour now helps to control the inflammation in your back as you grunt and limp along, nursing your lower back injury from Log PT twenty-four hours earlier.

Your team settles into a challenging but doable pace, as you snake your way south along the Coronado coast. The town of Tijuana, Mexico, only eight miles away, lights up the southern horizon and seems to extend out into the sea on the peninsula. After about a mile of running, you make the mistake of believing the moderate pace will last. Nothing moderate lasts when you are in hell. Lulled into complacency, you and the rest of the crew relax your pace to a limping, torturous centipede-like jog.

You soon realize you were very wrong to take your lead for granted. Do not take anything for granted in hell. Complacency is a SEAL killer.

Shouting can be heard behind your boat as the instructors suddenly start harassing a boat crew farther down the line.

The shouting gets closer and closer, until a boat crew goes sprinting up the line past your crew at a murderous pace. It sounds like drums are being played while men are tortured. The cries and grunts of pain and agony are louder than usual, as the boat slams up and down on their heads. Directly behind the crew, a SEAL shoves the boat forward, forcing the team to sprint to the front of the line.

Suddenly, the second boat crew passes your boat. Your crew seems shocked and awed as instructors push a third and a fourth past you. You had the lead and you are now getting your asses handed to you.

"They're about to hit us next!" you yell at your boat crew, aware that Price should be taking command. Aside from speaking to the instructor about the missing man, Ensign Price has remained silent during this whole ordeal thus far, and has not shown any leadership. He's clearly near a personal breaking point, perhaps very sick. He had complained of VGE. You tell yourself, *Help this man, don't quit on him.* And so you take up some of the leadership slack.

You can sense the instructors gaining. "Get ready to run!" you yell.

A light suddenly flashes behind you as an instructor runs up behind the boat. "You're goddamn right you're next!" the instructor barks. Without warning, he shoves your boat forward and the weight shifts on your heads, cutting flesh in new spots as you struggle to stay under the boat. "Run!"

Disorienting pain pulses through your head and neck as

the boat violently bounces on the top of your fucking skull. Sand continues to tear away at your scalp like a cheese grater on your crown as you run, and you fight to keep your feet moving, lifting each foot above the soft sand as fast as you can, so you can run. But it feels like you are running in quicksand, getting deeper with every step. The only remedy is to run faster.

Ensign Price slips and his body falls back through the legs of the centipede, threatening to bring everyone down, "Jesus! Look out!" The crew and boat almost crash. You reach down, pull him to his feet, and shove him forward. He recovers and so does the rest of the crew.

Collectively, you build speed, and your group sprints past the other crews straight toward the taillights of the pickup truck. The truck meanders down the beach, casually swerving back and forth, rubber tires spitting sand. It looks like the driver is drunk, enjoying a cold one as he torments a class of aspiring SEALs. You reach the truck and are rewarded for your effort with a lungful of diesel exhaust. The vile, bluish exhaust burns your chest and makes you lightheaded. You cough and retch violently, still trying to maintain a normal running pace. Heads spinning and gasping for air, the group trudges forward behind the truck until another crew comes shooting up the side, takes the lead, and settles in line in front of yours.

This process of taking, losing, and retaking the lead repeats itself dozens of times as your class continues running down the beach with fucking boats on their heads. Eventually, breakdowns happen. You see boat crews stumble and crash to the ground, frustrated and feebly enraged. You see spots of blood smeared on shaven heads, desperate faces, veins in necks bulging, all futilely. Men run out from under their boats and quit right in the middle of the sprint, forcing the rest of the crews to continue with less men. And then you hear whimpering near you, from under your boat.

You strain to listen in order to identify who is moaning—it's Price. Again. He slumps his head down and whimpers, snot streaming down his face. It's pathetic. Worse, as he slumps his head forward, the rest of the weight transfers to the rest of your group—already down a man. This maneuver, which is quite cowardly, is called "boat ducking."

"You better carry your fucking weight, you goddamn pussy!" one of the increasingly frustrated men in your crew screams at Ensign Price.

"I'm sick, I just can't," Price blubbers through his whimpers.

"Then fucking quit!" someone snaps.

"Nooooo," Ensign Price moans, almost bursting into tears.

You have seen enough men break to know the signs, and you believe Ensign Price is on the verge of DOR-ing. But you know it's only two days in and he has more to give. He's not done physically—far from it. And fundamentally, you don't want him to quit. You want him—you want every man—to stay, especially an officer. You tell yourself that if he quits, it means you and the rest of the crew quit on him. You suddenly feel that keeping Ensign Price with your crew is a noble goal.

You can't let him down. You won't desert this man. So you call out to him, "Hang in there, brother. Just keep fighting."

Someone else yells, "Fuckin' quit, pussy!"

You snarl back, "No! Shut the fuck up! Price is not quitting and if I hear anyone fucking calling him out, I'll kick your ass."

Your voice echoes in the cold night. The words and your ferocity startle you. You can feel the crew listening to you in the silence. And for a few minutes, they are kept at bay. By the force of your will, you convinced the boat crew to quiet their gripes against Price. Then he starts boat ducking again, moaning and acting very sick.

After six miles of running down the beach with each man effectively carrying the boat for Price so he can stumble underneath it, moan, and recover strength, the instructors order the class to stop and raise the boats above your heads with your arms. One crew at a time is given six seconds to run to a table that has been set up with Styrofoam cups filled with Gatorade while the rest of the crews hold the boats up above their heads.

When your crew's turn comes, each man grabs two cups and drinks it as fast as he can. Because you are sick and want to keep the Gatorade down, you try to sip it as slowly as you can without looking like you're trying to sneak in an extra break.

Although you are still dry heaving on occasion, you only ever actually vomit up material right after eating or drinking. Not all of it, though. You are able to keep down about a third of what you eat or drink, if you consume water or food slowly.

That said, anytime you eat or drink, especially drink, something is coming up and you puke.

In order to stay hydrated you have to sip slowly from a cup, taking tiny amounts of water into your mouth and slowly swallowing so the liquid dribbles inoffensively down your throat. It's like you're sucking water through a wet rag when you're dying of thirst—quite literally you are medically dehydrated from all the diarrhea and exertion. You are more dehydrated than you have ever been in your life. The way you crave water yet can't drink is similar to what it might be like to try breathing through a cocktail straw while running a marathon in August, in a really hot place. You need the water to live, and yet you must limit how much you drink to keep it from coming back up, which is maddening when your salted body is overcome with thirst.

You look over at Price, downing his Gatorade in a huge chug. This is not how someone with VGE should drink. It'll make him puke if he's sick, and if he pukes up what he's drinking it'll only make him weaker. "Ensign Price," you tell him, "if you drink too fast, you're going to puke. Slow it down."

He scowls at you like a drunken frat boy being told to sip a beer—an indignant arrogant smirk. "I'm good, dude." And he pounds his second cup. "You need to hurry up."

Okay...now there is no question about what is going on. He's boat ducking. And now you know, without any doubt, he has been faking being sick. He does not have VGE, nor any other ailment. It's all been a strategy, you realize. He's stalling to make it easier on himself. Being sick is one thing; faking sick so your crew has to pick up the slack for you is another.

"Ten seconds!" an instructor screams at your crew.

You throw your cups into a black garbage bag and then sprint back to pick up the goddamn boat.

"Land portage!" an instructor yells and the crews start running.

Once again, Price is moaning, boat ducking. You can hear him whining, "Oh...Jesus...I'm gonna puke. Help me."

"Fuck you, you bitch," someone yells. You feel the boat slow.

Worse than failing to lead and inspiring the crew, Price has become a shirker. His presence is creating only resentment. It is clear to you that his failure to lead and his unwillingness to take personal responsibility has become a liability for the rest of the crew. This has to end now, you tell yourself, or none of you are going to make it.

"Ensign Price!" you yell. "Either you stop boat ducking, or we are gonna run you out of this crew."

"Please," he whines, looking you in the eyes, begging. "Don't. Help me. Just slow down."

Like hell, you think, feeling a surge of unremorseful energy, *time to run this fucker out*. You speed up. "Dude, you need to quit now," you tell your former leader. "This isn't for you."

Lesson:

Being a SEAL requires that you never leave a fellow brother behind, that you carry the weight of others. And yet an important part of the SEAL training, a very harsh part, is letting go of whatever holds you back, which could be a behavior or a person who does not deserve to be part of your team.

There is a difference between quitting and letting go—a very important difference. The SEALs never quit, they never quit on themselves or their team, their brothers, those who are mentally committed to the same goals and objectives. But when someone is poisonous, selfish, who is just a drag and playing upon your sympathy, SEALs cut them loose. Let them do what they want—let them *try* to take the easy way out of hell.

The truth, however, is there is no easy way out of hell. Those whom you let quit because they are pulling you down will get the momentary relief they seek. They will get handed the coffee and blanket. The SEALs who want to stay in hell, who want to fight their way through hell and not cheat their way out, will never let you down. Don't let go of these people. Let go of the others, and the true warriors will thrive.

In life these are the coworkers who talk a good game but never commit, the people who say they want to help you but in the end only hurt you. You know who these people are. They are the ones who play on your sympathies, who suck the most of your energy and never give back. They only give excuses. Let them go.

The men of the team are ultimately responsible for the success or failure of the mission. When one man is unable to carry out that mission during training/qualification, what good will he be in battle? Not only will he compromise his own effectiveness, but he will compromise every man on the team in the event he must be helped and/or extracted (carried) from the field of battle. This is different from the ethos of "leave no man behind." Instead it is the understanding that if he is willing to quit during training, and thereby compromise the team, he will also be willing to quit during operations, where far more is at stake. Even after you are a member of the SEALs and have received your trident, you are still evaluated by your reputation (your "rep"), and every SEAL has one.

I'm reminded of the life, and ultimate death in battle, of SEAL Michael Monsoor. Michael was killed when he jumped on a grenade that had been thrown at him and his teammates in Iraq. Even though he could have easily gotten away from the blast and saved himself, he chose to cover the grenade and thereby attempt to save the lives of the other men on his team. The following is a copy of the citation that led to his posthumously receiving the Medal of Honor, our nation's highest award for gallantry:

For conspicuous gallantry and intrepidity at the risk of his life above and beyond the Call of Duty while serving as Automatic Weapons Gunner for Naval Special Warfare Task Group Arabian Peninsula, in support of

Operation IRAQI FREEDOM on 29 September 2006. As a member of a combined SEAL and Iraqi Army sniper overwatch element, tasked with providing early warning and stand-off protection from a rooftop in an insurgent-held sector of Ar Ramadi, Iraq, Petty Officer Monsoor distinguished himself by his exceptional bravery in the face of grave danger. In the early morning, insurgents prepared to execute a coordinated attack by reconnoitering the area around the element's position. Element snipers thwarted the enemy's initial attempt by eliminating two insurgents. The enemy continued to assault the element, engaging them with a rocket-propelled grenade and small arms fire. As enemy activity increased, Petty Officer Monsoor took position with his machine gun between two teammates on an outcropping of the roof. While the SEALs vigilantly watched for enemy activity, an insurgent threw a hand grenade from an unseen location, which bounced off Petty Officer Monsoor's chest and landed in front of him. Although only he could have escaped the blast, Petty Officer Monsoor chose instead to protect his teammates. Instantly and without regard for his own safety, he threw himself onto the grenade to absorb the force of the explosion with his body, saving the lives of his two teammates. By his undaunted courage, fighting spirit, and unwavering devotion to duty in the face of certain death, Petty Officer Monsoor gallantly gave his

life for his country, thereby reflecting great credit upon
himself and upholding the highest traditions of the
United States Naval Service.

We all will limp along. We all need a hand at some point.
We all suck at some point. But men like Michael Monsoor
don't boat duck. SEALs don't. And those who habitually do so
deserve to be cut loose.

If you want to survive hell, learn to let go but never quit.

CHAPTER 6

If you want to survive hell, don't hesitate to take charge.

In the absence of orders, I will take charge, lead my teammates and accomplish the mission.

—Navy SEAL Creed

We don't give a shit. You just better carry your weight," one man in the team tells Price.

"I will. I am with you boys." He acts like he's going to pick up the slack, and maybe some of the guys think he will, but you know better. Not even a quarter mile later you hear the familiar whimpering start again. Price is bent over, boat ducking, the strain is felt, and the weight of his shirking is borne by the entire crew.

Someone needs to cut this damn cord, you tell yourself.

"Price," you hear yourself saying, "you're fucking boat ducking. You either need to carry your weight or quit."

"I can't. I can't do this," he says. "I'm gonna puke. I can feel it."

"You lying bastard," you say. "You're not sick. If you want to quit, then just quit."

"What did I just hear?" You hear a voice. You look to see

Joker running beside the boat. "Did you just tell your boat leader to quit?"

You say nothing.

"I fucking love it! Run that pussy out of the group. He's worthless. He's worse than worthless, he's fucking dangerous." Other instructors hear this and come running along. They know your crew has turned on its leader for weakness, and they love it. They are like a pack of hyenas. "Price," they yell, "quit, man!"

"Cry your sorry ass to sleep back in the barracks! Quit, you pussy!"

Joker starts a cheer: "Run him out! Run him out! Run him out!"

This is a normal occurrence in BUD/S when a team recognizes that an individual is mentally breaking down and hurting the rest of the team by not carrying his weight, but Joker seems to be reveling in it more than most. He loves this. He's running next to Price, who is now in full tears-and-slobber mode. Joker yells, "He's crying! He's crying! Hahaha."

You know it is common for a crew to expel a person on the verge of quitting, either by physically pushing him away from the team and refusing to let him participate, or by running at a punishing pace that he can't keep up with. But Price is still hanging in; at least his feet are moving. Another godawful two miles or so, and you finally reach the end of a three-mile run. You are nearly back at the base, can see the entrance. All you want is some other exercise, anything to get the boat off your heads. You pull up and stop. "Down boat," you are told by an instructor. You put the boat down and wait for directions.

"I'm good now," Price tells the crew, sucking wind, hands on hips. "I'm better."

Of course you're better, you're resting, you want to say.

Then the truck pulls up. "Oh, I'll bet you guys thought we were done, didn't you?" Joker says over the megaphone. "Up boat! Prepare for land portage. We're doing it again!"

Price's shoulders slump forward as he halfheartedly helps pick up the boat. "Goddamn Price, start pulling your weight," someone says. "I can see you boat ducking, dude. Man up!"

"But I'm sick," he says again as the group builds to a run. "Guys, help me out. I'll be good in a bit." If he was sick or injured, the group probably would have slowed down a bit and taken the extra beatings to protect him.

On more than one occasion in the past twenty-four hours, the crew has suffered for your sickness and injury, and you have tried to pick up the slack for Price, believing, however doubtfully, that he might have been sick. No one wants to turn on a teammate who gives their all, sick or not. Everyone knows there may be a moment when someone has to take up their slack. No one wants to see a good dude fail. But you and the group all know your supposed boat crew "leader" is lying, while boat ducking and holding you back. No more mercy.

The race back down the beach in the dark begins in earnest once again. A constant stream of curses and insults flies at Price. The instructors harass everyone sprinting down the dark beach. Your crew is again badgered because you have fallen behind due to Price's bullshit. They're screaming, "Price, you pussy, hurry up!" "Stop ducking this shit!" There's a lot of talk. But Price is still there. He's dragging ass, slowing the crew down.

Finally, you have had enough. You decide to take charge. "Everyone shut the fuck up!" you scream at your crew. At barely nineteen years old you are by far the youngest on the team, and the sudden outburst surprises them and they stop talking. "We're going to run him out of the crew!"

"YES!" the instructors scream at the entire group. "YESSSS!"

"Let's do it!" one of the other men yells.

"Go! Go! Go!" you scream. The guys at the front of the crew angle the group out of line and begin sprinting forward up the line of other crews.

The SEAL instructors laugh hysterically and run alongside your crew, cheering you on and screaming at your leader. "Ensign Price, quit! Quit, sir! Hahaha." They mock his rank.

The group reaches the front of the line and continues chasing after the truck at full speed. Your legs feel like lead and your neck feels as if it could snap at any second. But you do not break your stride.

"Slow down," Price commands, trying to regain authority. "Slow down, guys. That's an order! I'm fine!"

Yeah, you know he's fine. And that's the problem. He's physically fine. Not mentally, not morally.

Another boat crew comes running up beside yours, attempting to get in front. "Keep going! Faster!" you scream, knowing the other crew will force you to slow down if they get ahead of you. The boat crew races ahead. And though your heart is pumping, it is at this peak effort that the boat feels the lightest. It is at this moment that you feel yourself and the crew hit stride, with everyone running at their full effort. Everyone but one.

"Aghghhhhhhhh." Price lets out a high-pitched cry, staggers, then bashes his head against the bottom of the boat. You watch as he quite literally jumps away from the boat. He falls to the ground. The weight of the boat hardly shifts, confirming that he hadn't been carrying his weight anyway. The SEAL instructors swarm him, kicking sand in his face. You and your crew continue running, as you glance back. The instructors surround him, Joker leading the pack. They look demonic. Price covers up, shrieking. This is the last time you see Ensign Price.

Down to only five men and utterly exhausted from the extreme effort, your crew begins to falter and fall behind the others. The SEAL instructors show no mercy as they harass your crew for being slow, but the derision and disgust in their voices have been replaced with a matter-of-fact tone as they "inform" the group that just because you are down men, that does not excuse anyone for failing to keep up.

It is apparent that you are now the leader of the crew, and, having expelled a bad member of your team, the group now functions like clockwork. At your command, each man seamlessly rotates positions under the boat to take turns in the more difficult positions, and each man carries his fair share of the weight. For the next two miles, the team struggles along in the cold, dark sand together until you reach the rest of the class and tables where you are able to drink.

Other crews are in similar predicaments of being undermanned and in utter misery. But as some men quit, others take charge and lead their crews.

Collectively the disheveled mass forms another height line on the beach and reestablishes new boat crews of seven men each. You find yourself in a new crew with a new boat crew leader and settle back into your role as follower, ready to take charge again if necessary. Little do you know that this is the essence of the SEAL Teams.

Lesson:

To be a SEAL and to survive in the hardest times, you must be able to adapt to the situation and accomplish your mission, even when this means doing the difficult thing of running someone out of your crew. It has to be done, but who will step up and take charge? That person is you.

A portion of the Navy SEAL Creed says it best: "We expect to lead and be led. In the absence of orders I will take charge, lead my teammates and accomplish the mission. I lead by example in all situations."

Take charge, don't be afraid to evolve and change who you are, and don't let others' past expectations of you dictate your future. Team-ability, adaptability—you can't do it alone. Others need you too. Break out of your comfort zone and adapt who you are.

Leaders naturally gravitate toward the challenge. Even in failure, they are looked upon as ones who did everything they could to win. This is the quality respected in life. And these people in the teams eventually do win.

In life, like in the teams, during the most difficult times we will see an opportunity to step up and lead, even if we are not naturally leaders. When we see the way forward, we must act, we must change in order to succeed and overcome. This is about stepping up in these insane situations. You *can* lead. You *will* lead if you overcome fear and doubt and speak up. And best of all, you will feel yourself begin to change. You will recognize qualities and strengths in yourself you did not realize you had. They come out when you act. Stop thinking, take the lead.

> During Hell Week, the focus is on survival—students demonstrating they have what it takes to get through this incredibly difficult training cycle. We don't expect much in terms of quality of performance or leadership during this week, but when we see it, it is noted. So, when a kid, especially an enlisted kid still in his teens, shows he can lead during Hell Week, you know you have the makings of an exceptional SEAL candidate and human.
>
> —Ed Hiner, Navy SEAL retired lieutenant commander and BUD/S instructor

CHAPTER 7

DAY THREE

If you want to survive hell, beware of momentary comfort and don't ever let your guard down.

My Nation expects me to be physically harder and mentally stronger than my enemies. If knocked down, I will get back up every time.

—Navy SEAL Creed

Your arms shake and your back sags from exhaustion as you attempt to keep yourself in the push-up position with your feet up on the side of your boat. After two full nights of unrelenting punishment, everyone's bodies begin to quite literally break down—your muscles are in a catabolic state, the fibers and proteins that make up your muscles are being broken down and torn apart. With proper rest and diet, you'd be packing on hard muscle and shedding fat. Now your body is consuming over 10,000 calories a day, far more energy than you can possibly fuel with food. With little to no fat storage left in your body (yes, you are beyond shredded), your body is consuming energy wherever it can get it, including from the proteins stored in your muscles, which have been repeatedly beaten apart with constant strain and violent mechanical movement.

Many of your classmates have suffered serious injuries, severe strains, and deep tissue bruising. Some have small fractures, some have broken bones. All sailors are either very close to hypothermia or have the genuine article. A few of your classmates have contracted pneumonia, and maybe one among the group has or will develop life-threatening internal bleeding. Everyone looks beat up, sunburnt, scraped raw, covered in blisters and gashes. Many of these cuts and scrapes are infected. And of course, there is VGE and a host of other ailments ravaging the class.

Because you and your class are so jacked up, there is no way instructors or corpsmen trailing you can spot a candidate in danger among the herd. You need to slow down and have a medical professional take a closer look. The difference between a sailor whose ass is kicked to shit and the sailor whose life is in danger is not always apparent visually. So you and the rest of your class need to be inspected by a medic.

On Tuesday afternoon you are about to receive your first "break" since starting Hell Week. This break consists of five minutes one-on-one with a Navy doctor to make sure you didn't have any threat to "life, limb, or eyesight."

One by one, boat crews put their feet down and file out of

the training area, cross over a giant sand berm, and run into a medical building, momentarily released for medical checks. While aspiring SEALs go in to see the docs in groups of seven at a time, the rest of the class waits in the "leaning rest" position.

An instructor cautions your class, "If any one of you takes more than the allotted five minutes with the doctor and he doesn't diagnose you with a major health issue and pull you from training, we will single you out and crush you." He says this as he walks past sand-caked, shaking human forms lined up in a shivering row. You have heard that guys will feign injury and have the doctors check every joint and muscle in an attempt to game the system and get an extended respite from hell. And you have heard what happens to these men. The instructors, of course, can sniff out the fakers and gamers and, as you just heard, crush them. Projecting weakness, even when injury or sickness is present, is not allowed in a SEAL candidate. They only want men who will willingly suffer through hardship. But you have also heard that it doesn't matter. "You're either gonna be the kind who makes it, or the kind who quits." The ones who game the system are really gaming themselves and will DOR.

"Boat Crew Five! You're up next!" The instructor calls your crew number.

As quickly as your group can, all seven of you recover from "resting" position and jump to your feet. You stow your life jackets, helmets, and paddles inside the boat while the SEAL instructor screams, "Faster! Faster! Move your fucking asses!"

Candidates are not allowed to run through the gaps in the twelve-foot sand berm. So you and your team scramble over the top and sprint down into the parking lot of the medical facility. Standing in the parking lot, a new batch of SEAL instructors bark orders. Joker paces out front, his scarred face clean-shaven, glistening, and mean.

"You disgusting slackers will find two buckets with your names on them," Joker says, and you swear he looks up, locks eyes with you, and continues. "Pussies," he says, staring at you. "Take all of your piss- and shit-stained clothes off except your skivvies and put the clothes in the empty bucket. In the second bucket you will find a clean, dry uniform."

You recognize the buckets. Before Hell Week started you were given two empty five-gallon buckets and were told to label them with your name. In one bucket you were instructed to place an extra uniform, T-shirt, and socks. The other bucket was to remain empty. This empty bucket is the one you now put your dirty clothes into. Standing by to assist in this work are a crew of pre–Hell Week BUD/S. These are students called "White Shirts." You were a White Shirt a few weeks ago, so you know the drill. The White Shirts will take the dirty clothes and wash them, so everyone has clean uniforms ready for medical checks the next day. When you are sent into the medical check, you will be instructed to change from your dirty uniform into the clean one. The purpose of wearing a clean uniform each day is to prevent the spread of bacteria and fungus, which so easily grow in wet environments and infect bodies that have multiple open wounds and compromised immune systems. Also, there are no official bathroom breaks during Hell Week, so as Joker referenced, everyone urinates on themselves, and every class has a few guys who shit themselves. This makes the uniforms even more toxic.

"Hurry the fuck up!" Joker yells. You find your bucket and with shaking hands and numb fingers unbutton your excrement- and vomit-soaked uniform. You place the dirty clothes in the empty bucket and put your sandy, soaked boots next to the bucket filled with water and your clean uniform. You gaze at the dry uniform; putting it on after the medical check will be like slipping into heaven, if only for a minute.

Joker then yells, "Before you get your ass checked out, wait for me. I am gonna pay you a friendly medical visit of my own." He signals a fellow instructor to bring him a garden hose. Cold clear water pumps out of its end, splattering all over the concrete. Joker whistles and sings as he walks along the line of buckets: "*Zip-a-dee-doo-dah, zip-a-dee-ay, My, oh my, what a wonderful day, Plenty of sunshine headin' my way!*" Cackling, Joker then sprays water into the buckets containing the clean, dry uniforms, filling each bucket so every fiber of clothing is soaked. "You all thought you'd be fucking airing your balls out in there while you play pocket pool with the docs. No chance. Being dry, even for a millisecond, is not allowed during *my* Hell Week.

"Okay, go see the corpsmen," Joker instructs. "And you have five minutes!"

Barefoot, shivering, and wearing nothing by skivvies, you stand in line behind a few other students waiting your turn. While in line you can't help but look at the bodies of the other men. The sight is horrible. You realize you aren't the only one suffering from sickness and injury. Standing on the firm concrete, as opposed to soft sand, you realize the extent of your back injury is even worse than you had initially thought. Merely standing on the concrete exacerbates the pain shooting through your spine.

Massive blisters mark the feet of most of the men, while raw open wounds from the sandy chafing can be seen on almost every candidate. Many limp from swollen joints, ankles, and knees, and some cough uncontrollably from a rare kind of pneumonia the trainees call "sipe." Sipe only occurs in climbers attempting to summit Mount Everest—and in students attempting to make it through Navy SEAL training.

You are no medic, but you can tell a few guys have sipe. One of them hangs his head low and tries to muffle his coughing to downplay his illness. This man wants to stay. Another man hacks and coughs and convulses like he's a sick dad in a Mucinex commercial. This sailor clearly wants an excuse to get dropped or rolled back without being forced to publicly quit.

"Next!" a corpsman yells.

You walk into the medical exam room and sit down on a table. On similar tables around the room, another four or five other students also sit while being examined by the medical staff. You have never been so happy to be in a medical facility. It is warm and dry, no one is screaming at you, and you actually get to sit on a padded table. Cold plastic never felt so good under your ass.

The corpsman, an enlisted medic, walks over to you and takes your vital signs. He then listens to your lungs as a doctor checks you over for infections and injuries.

The doc pokes and prods tender areas of your body—your arms, legs, back, joints, all the while watching you closely for a pain response. "Are you feeling any severe pain?" the doctor asks as his gloved fingers push and pull your skin.

"Nope," you say, and you want to laugh out loud. The question is absurdly dumb. Clearly, the doc has never been through Hell Week.

"Are you able to keep food and water down?"

"Yep," you lie. Though your VGE has gotten a little less severe, you have been puking and plagued by diarrhea since Hell Week started. You are not trying to be a hero or a tough guy by lying to the doctor about your sickness. You are being practical about future torture. You have made it to Tuesday afternoon of Hell Week, and although you continue to deteriorate and weaken, you believe you at least have a fighting chance of making it through to the end. And you have no intention of ever repeating a single second of this training.

The doctor moves his spidery hands over to your back and

checks your lower spine for injuries. When he presses lightly with his fingers, you suddenly flinch in pain. His hands freeze in place and he looks up at you. "Did that hurt?"

"What?"

"I touched the area around your lower lumbar spine and you spasmed, quite noticeably."

"I'm just a little sore."

He pushes his glasses up on his nose, watching you. "Sailor, back injuries are not a joke, we should maybe get an X-ray."

"No, no, no sir," you say, barely able to keep your voice controlled and not shout. If you get an X-ray or miss more than two hours of Hell Week for a medical check, you will automatically be pulled from the class and have to start from the beginning with the next class. "I really am fine. I'm just sore."

He scowls. "You could do permanent damage to yourself, maybe cripple yourself, if you have an undiagnosed spinal fissure. An X-ray will resolve that."

"I'm good, just sore."

He lets out a long sigh and shakes his head with a shrug, clearly baffled as to why you would refuse the help.

"Okay, then," he says, "you're free to go. But if that back gets worse, you need to tell us."

"Roger that, sir! Thank you, sir!" You hobble out of the medical building as fast as your cramping legs will carry you, all the while vowing that you will never talk to that doctor again. As you make it to the door you look back at the men from your boat crew who had come in with you. One remains sitting on a padded table. He was the sailor who had been dramatically hacking and coughing. A heated blanket is wrapped over his shoulders. His body looks blue and his muscles and frame shiver. He looks very cold and ill indeed. He is being taken to get a chest X-ray. A doctor is telling him that after he's treated, he can continue training with the next class. He's nodding, saying, "I just want to get back out there." Then he looks up at you, your eyes meet, and you can read the fear and shame that race through him. The look in his posture and in his eyes tell you he's quit. He caved. And he knows you know it. How did it happen? You went to the doctor to get checked out, not to check in and never leave. So what happened? The kid was extremely cold. He sat on the table, got a taste of warmth, and let the doctors talk him into quitting on himself. Again, he knows you know.

You turn, hustle out the door to the parking lot where Joker is standing immediately outside the door, as if he's waiting for you and you alone. "Oh, motherfucker? Is that what you want? I see. You want pain. Good. Roger that!" He screams at you and sprays you with ice-cold water as you head to the balled-up, soaking-wet uniform in your bucket. You had just gotten warm enough to really feel the cold from the hose. It hurts more because of your "break."

Joker continues to spray you in the face as you try to put on the freezing, soaking uniform. "Looks like someone decided they wanted to take some extra time with the doctor! You were in there for fifteen minutes!"

You know what he said is not at all true. You had gone in and out of that stupid medical facility faster than most of the other guys in your crew, and there was no way in hell it had been fifteen minutes. Joker is singling you out because he likes to fuck with you, he wants you to hurt so badly that you quit. That will never happen.

"Hurry up! Hurry up!" he screams at you as you try to work your wet T-shirt over your head. "Oh, look at this! You want to take your time with the doc, *and* you want to take your time getting dressed! Seems to me you don't want to be here!"

You do your best to ignore him and the deluge of freezing water that blinds you. *Let's get this shit over with,* you are saying to yourself. *Fuck the breaks. Just keep it coming.*

Lesson:

Every hurricane has an eye. In the middle of a horrible life-threatening storm, there is a spot of calm, of bright warm light. A surreal reprieve in the middle of hell when we are tempted to think the storm has passed. We relax, let our guard down, and perhaps even believe the storm really has passed. But then the black clouds return, the storm closes in around us and mercilessly demolishes our homes and demoralizes us.

We curse the eye of the storm as a cruel trick, and yet many of us try to live our lives chasing it, constantly trying to stay in the calm center of an otherwise terrifying event. We seek out shortsighted momentary wins, but lose the greater battle. We work hard at our jobs to be complimented, then relax instead of working harder. We get a pat on the back, but lose the promotion. Lawyers have a good day in court, feel confident, and then fail to prepare for the next day and get their asses handed to them. A salesman in a slump has a good few days, splurges on drinks with his clients, and then misses his monthly quota.

For SEALs, medical checks exist to save lives by screening for very serious problems that can develop. They are also a tool to encourage the uncommitted to drop out while supposedly keeping their dignity. The opposite is true. In fact, most SEALs have more respect for the sailor who quits in front of his class than the one who weasels out of the program with a medical issue that he could have fought through.

And yet the eye of the storm is seductive. When we feel

the warmth, we all are tempted to linger, but just remember the eye never lasts. When you walk back out into real life and get sprayed in the face with ice-cold water, you will feel it more painfully. Do not use the momentary reprieve in the battle as an excuse to rest. Make use of the time to batten down the hatches. When you are given a breather and have a chance to quit or give in to temptation, use the time to mentally recommit.

> You get killed when you let your guard down. This is true in life and in war. In life, you get killed when you get on the expressway and space out. The most dangerous times during a mission are when there is a lull in the fight, when a dynamic changes, when there is a gap in focus. That is when mistakes are made or the enemy does something unexpected. Continuity of focus is so important. The normal work-up time leading up to a deployment, in other words the time SEALs spend training for deployment, is twelve to eighteen months. Think about that. SEALs will take a year and a half of hard, continuous training to prepare for the time they go to war. During Hell Week, which is unbelievably intense, any pause in training is a chance to lose focus, to make a mistake, to give in to the temptation to quit. Keep your head in the game, always.
> —Chris Sajnog, SEAL instructor

If you want to survive hell, beware of momentary comfort and don't ever let your guard down.

PART III

TIME IN HELL IS RELATIVE AND VERY LONG

CHAPTER 8

DAY THREE

If you want to survive hell, it pays to be a winner.

The five-gallon bucket, half full of ice water and your *clean* uniform, awaits you. You pull the clothes out, peel them open, wring some of the water out, and put them on. After donning your wet uniform, you assume the "leaning rest" position and wait for the last remaining member of your boat crew, your swim buddy, to finish his inspection, dress, and line up next to you. During BUD/S you are never supposed to be more than a few paces from your swim buddy. A swim buddy is a dynamic thing; he is sometimes assigned during an exercise, but more generally is the closest trainee to you. Today he's a kid from Ohio, a short, stocky, religious, somewhat innocent twenty-year-old kid named Marcos. You have a feeling Marcos will make it. He's one of those innocent aw-shucks kind of guys, but there's also an element of crazy-ass lead-slinger in him. The quiet, shy ones are the most nuts.

And he's tough. He's never the fastest, never the best, but he's a no-quit motherfucker. The reason why the doctors are taking so long is it's pretty clear he's got pneumonia and they are giving him an even closer look than they gave you.

As soon as Marcos is ready, together you run back over the berm to join your class on the beach. "What kind of games were you playing in there?" Joker runs over and gets in your face. "I don't want to see you slacking anymore! Believe me, you don't want to slack anymore," he keeps yelling after you as you charge up the berm. Then comes that one word loaded with pain. "Drop!"

Both of you drop into push-up position. "Not you, Marcos, get your fucking ass up!" Joker kicks sand into your face. "You fucking slacker. I want to see two hundred push-ups, now!" You start pushing them out, feet up, face down, still on the berm. "No more slacking," Joker continuously repeats, kicking a giant clump of sand into your face. It gets in your eyes and mouth and lungs. He keeps kicking until you finish all two hundred push-ups. "Now hustle your asses back to the beach!"

"What did you do?" Marcos asks, running next to you, as soon as Joker is out of earshot.

"Absolutely nothing," you say and want to add, *Joker is just a fucking sadistic asshole*. But Marcos does not use *cuss words*, and in any case, in his pure Baptist heart, you don't need to tell him because he knows Joker is a cocksucking d-bag.

When all of the medical checks are complete, and the entire remaining class has assembled on the beach, you are ordered to pick up your boats and carry them to the obstacle course. At the O Course, you notice several dozen rucksacks, all lined up in a neat row right outside the entrance of the Trail of Tears, the soft sand "jogging" trail that snakes through the training facility. Running on this trail, while wet and sandy and in the broiling sun, is a mild yet effective form of slow torture that has been known to fell many a strong-willed man.

"Listen up, gentlemen," Joker says into the megaphone. "The next thing you're going to do is go for a little ruck run, a short jog. And I expect no one to fall behind. No excuses or exceptions will be tolerated." He takes a drink from a frosty bottle of water. We gawk and salivate, our mouths perpetually dry and caked with grit. "Since you've all had a nice, leisurely break for medical inspection, and since the docs have given you all a gleaming clean-ass bill of health, if you fall behind, we will know that you are faking it—" (This, of course, is nonsense. Fully a quarter of the remaining men in the class are either significantly sick or injured, which is enough to slow you down, but not enough to be removed from training.) "—and if you get caught faking it, you will be severely punished." Joker drains the plastic water bottle and tosses it into the back of the pickup. The crinkling sound of the light plastic thud makes your mouth scream for water. "This will be an individual exercise. You are not working as teams. No fuckbuddies, no swim buddies either. As I said, if you fall behind, you will be punished. And"—he smiles a full cat grin, savoring the moment—"if you slow down to help anyone who has fallen behind, you will be punished. And not only will we give you a beatdown, by me personally, but we will also punish the person you are trying to help, even more than we would for just being a slacking piece of shit. We want to see who the winners in this group are and who the losers are. You will be judged on your time. And this judge"—Joker points to himself—"is fucking hardcore. Am I clear?"

A weak "Hooyah, Instructor" is all the enthusiasm the class can muster. It is one thing to compete with groups of students, where each man has a team to support him as he contends with his classmates—all extremely motivated, highly competitive, and competent aspiring Navy SEALs. It is quite another thing for each man to compete with every man for himself and against that same class. It is a brawl of wills, fought on the Trail of Tears.

"Everyone ruck up!" an instructor yells.

You race your classmates over to the line of ragged, tattered rucksacks. The rucks, of course, like everything else during Hell Week, are soaking wet and covered with sand. Inside each rucksack sits a fifty-pound bag of sand, tightly wrapped in duct tape, forming a large medicine ball. Your muscles are frayed, extremely stiff from just a few moments of inaction, and your entire body hurts. You strain to lift the ruck onto your back and tighten down the shoulder straps, feeling the sand stuck to the back of the ruck cut into your skin. *Let the chafing begin.*

"Line up facing south!" an instructor commands.

Your feet slip as you try to run through the soft sand behind a throng of other students, all trying to push toward the front so they can start at the head of the pack. Before the class is lined up, however, a truck filled with SEALs shoots past and guns it down the trail. A SEAL calls from the flatbed, "You turds better keep up!"

A full third of the students have yet to get their rucks on their backs when you suddenly begin running south. You look back at your classmates struggling with their gear and to catch up. Your instinct is to wait and encourage them, especially Marcos, who had just been your swim buddy, but you must heed the order. Helping will only hurt you and them. So you turn to the south and focus only on catching the man in front of you. And beating him.

The sand underneath the shoulder straps and grating against your lower back really begins to saw away at your skin, and the shifting weight and bounces that accompany every step send terrible courses of nerve pain down your lower spine to your toes. Your legs feel like sandbags swinging from your torso as you catch the man in front of you. You hurl your legs one in front of the other and edge past him. For the first time at BUD/S you take the lead in the race. The feeling that accompanies this realization is both thrilling and terrifying. How are you going to keep up this pace? Will this draw attention to you? Will this create an unsustainable expectation? But it feels so good to lead. You are filled with glorious contradictions and confusion, and try to force these thoughts out of your head and just give your all. You hear an instructor berating the man behind you, and you press on.

Less than a mile later, you feel your body slowing down. Several men who had been running behind you are now running to your right and left. You strain your body to its fullest potential, and despite your efforts, they slowly slip forward, and you slip back. Instructors now are calling your name, chiding you. "Run, you fat motherfucker! Get back in the lead! Run!"

You try not to panic. You know the repercussions of falling behind. The instructors will stop you, make you do some kind of godawful exercise to weaken you even more, and then they will scream at you to catch up with the pack, tearing into your ass for letting the pack get ahead. The weaker and farther behind you get, the more you will fail to meet up with the pack, and then again you will be stopped by the instructors and the cycle will repeat itself. The rules governing this rat race are decidedly unfair. The weak only get weaker and are forced to fall farther behind, while those who can hold on to the lead get farther ahead. You damn well better stay at the front of the pack, you tell yourself. And you do.

After one and a half miles of running, the instructors stop the leaders and order you to turn around and run back the way you came, to the north. Running north, you pass the men, the losers, who have fallen behind. They are harassed by the SEAL instructors, forced to do calisthenics in the sand, forced to crawl—as always, sand is kicked in their faces—and they are kept from quickly reaching the turnaround point. Thank God you are with the leaders. No matter what happens, you can't let yourself fall into this group, no matter the cost. If you must push yourself to the point of collapse, that is preferable to being harassed by the instructors.

You can see ahead to the men who have passed you—five of them in total, maybe a hundred yards from the first man to you. As he crosses the finish line and reaches the starting point of the race, you can hear Joker ordering him to take off his rucksack and get water. The same happens with the next four men. You are a few paces behind the fifth man, who is Marcos. You are nearly running alongside him and well ahead of the men behind you, all of whom have fallen far to the rear. You do not have the heart to pass your friend, though you probably could if you needed to.

You let Marcos cross the line a few feet ahead of you, see him drop his ruck, and you feel the same relief as you step across the finish line, thanking God that you stayed at the front of the pack. You loosen the straps and start to drop your ruck. "Keep that goddamn pack on, pussy," Joker says, "and turn your ass around. Time to run the trail again."

You are floored. This does not make sense. You were right behind the fifth man, Marcos, who is gazing back at you, a worried look on his face. Then he turns and runs for the water. Joker sees you hesitate. "Are you disobeying me? Wipe that bitch-ass look off your fucking face and tell me right now—are you quitting?"

You are fully winded but manage to say, "No sir," as you start to turn around.

"I don't like your disobedient tone. Quit, you mother-fucker, or drop!"

You drop. Fifty push-ups later (with fifty pounds on your back), you scramble again to your feet and head back down the Trail of Tears, now far behind the leaders.

"It pays to be a winner!" Joker laughs. "Hahahahahaha! Lotto tickets for sale," he yells as he points down the trail, turning men around. "You assholes didn't want to put out, and that's fine. Now you're going to do it again. Run!"

Pissed off, you hustle back down the trail, passing some of the same men who had fallen far behind. They, of course, are being mercilessly harassed by the instructors. The sight reminds you of men running football drills, trying to get past defensemen. You watch one man break down into tears, fall to his knees, and drop his head. "Keep it up, buddy," you say, then instantly regret it, worried that the instructors might accuse you of helping the man and give you a beatdown. But they don't. They are having too much fun beating him down.

The SEAL instructors continue to laugh hysterically, con-tinue to kick sand into his face and demand that he quit. You hear him sobbing, "I will not." And you run on, out of earshot.

When you reach the turnaround point and start back to base for the second time, the teary-eyed student is no longer on the Trail of Tears. He has quit and has been removed from training, but the instructors never let up. They torture the other men who have fallen behind and who are now bear-crawling along the trail with their rucks.

"Hurry up, you turds!" the SEALs taunt. "This is what you get for falling behind. If you fall behind in war, you die, or worse yet, your buddy dies!"

After completing the run for a second time and having run six total miles, you now hope to be given a break with the other five men, but your Spidey sense tells you your favorite instructor, Joker, will order you to turn around and run the trail again.

And as you near what you hope will be the end of this cycle, you learn your instincts are...correct. Your Spidey sense is spot on. You are sent back by Joker. Worse, you see your buddy Marcos has been given a break. He's watching you and you want to hate him, but he holds up his fist when no one is looking and nods to you. *You got this*, he is saying. This powers you forward. Thank God for Marcos.

Three more miles later, you and the men running with you are finally ordered to take off your rucksacks and are allowed to drink. You chug the water as quickly as you can between heaving breaths, and without making yourself puke. You have only had two cups when you hear a familiar voice.

"Is everyone finished?" Joker says over the megaphone. "Good. Line up. And head south!"

The truck with the SEAL instructors peels out, kicking sand, and rumbles back down the Trail of Tears. "You better catch up!" the other SEALs scream.

Your legs nearly give out, and your heart feels as if it will stop. You can't believe you will be running down the mother-fucking trail for a fourth time in a row, albeit this time without rucksacks. In that moment, out of the corner of your eye you see two students suddenly break from the ranks, heads hanging low, and head for the bell. *Ding! Ding! Ding!* They've had enough.

"Hurry up!" instructors yell as they herd your group back toward the Trail of Tears.

"Moooo!" Someone in the front of the pack lets out a loud moan like a cow being led to slaughter.

"Who the fuck did that!?" an instructor screams.

"Moooo!" Another anonymous student calls out from somewhere else in the pack.

"Shut the goddamn fuck up, or I'll fucking destroy you all!" The veins bulge in Joker's neck, spittle flies.

"Moooo!"

"Moooo!"

A crescendo of anonymous mooing rises over the trail in defiance as your team lumbers down the soft sand rut as one unified pack.

You join in too. What more could they do to you?

Soon you will find out...

Lesson:

In life and in the SEALs, injustice, failed expectations, and empty promises are not just common—they are the rule. Life is *not* fair, ever. We all know Lady Luck is an unfair bitch. Both bad and good luck—physical health, athleticism, looks, wealth, where you stand in the path of a sniper's bullet—are doled out indiscriminately. In reality, often good luck goes to those who don't need it and the rest of us catch the shit and have to fight and scrap to get anywhere close to even. What is worse, when luck is taken out of the equation, when the field is as fair as possible, the rules of the game disproportionately favor the winners. This is really important to understand—life gives more good shit to winners and destroys losers, even the ones who are just a step or two behind the best of the best.

Those in the lead get rewarded and get ahead; those who struggle fall behind, and then they get their asses kicked so they fall further and further behind, until winning is hopeless, and you will never ever get a break until you can get ahead. This is not an aphorism that contains a truth—this is THE TRUTH. No matter how hard you work or deserving you are, the winners get paid. If you don't win, you don't get paid. You eat shit or, in the case of Hell Week, a boot full of sand.

You need to have a thick skin, perseverance, and a never-quit attitude in order to get by. But there comes a point in life and in hell and during Hell Week when simply limping along is a liability. The weak—the injured, the out of shape, the poor bastards with pneumonia and VGE—are the ones who are preyed upon and culled out of the herd. It's not their fault they got sick, but they lost all the same and the world pounced.

This is a very cruel truth about life that is deeply important to understand. When you are sick, suffering, and down and out you can NEVER count on getting a fucking break, and when you do it is pure luck, quite often the luck of where you were born and who you were born to. Most of us are not lucky. This is why you can never stop trying to win.

Life, at least in the United States, operates like the stock market. The stock market does not give a Wall Street trader who is down on his luck a break—ever. The trader eats what he kills, and the more he kills, the more he eats and the more he can kill. Or he goes fucking broke and into debt trying. The unlucky bastard who gets cancer also gets the medical bills, often loses his job or can't work, winds up broke, and if he's really unlucky, maybe he even gets left by his wife for a younger, healthier guy. Life is fucking unfair.

Countries, and the far leftist politicians in the United States, often try to level the playing field with the intention of giving the same, or similar, to all. This premise is at the heart of socialism and communism, and the truth is, once governments "level the playing field" and socialize, the ONLY ones who win are the thugs, bosses, and insiders. Look at Russia, Venezuela, Cuba, or AOC's inner circle.

Capitalistic democracies like the United States are rare. Life here can be ruthless, but it is the fairest system of them all. And you must, in any and all circumstances, fight your way to the front. Once you get to the front, you better fucking stay there, because as hard as it is to get to the front, it is much, much, much harder and much shittier to try to keep up, much less make up ground once you have fallen behind. Again, the race does not end when there is suffering. Marathons do not stop running when participants die of heatstroke or heart attacks, let alone when some poor bastard shits their pants or twists an ankle. In this race, if you slow down you will lose. And when your life hangs in the balance, losing cannot be an option. Let someone else die.

I repeat: Perseverance is the only way to combat and defeat injustice. Life's not fair, but mentally preparing for the unfairness will get you through. The fastest guys got to rest, while the slower ones were beaten more. "The rich get richer." Fight your way to the top. The cards may be stacked against you and life may suck, but don't give up. There is no individual, from billionaire to shoeshine stand operator, who has not failed and received injustice in the process. The billionaire generally just kept swinging.

The brotherhood among SEALs is unbelievably strong, stronger than any other on earth, I believe. And, counterintuitively, I think the reason for this is that as SEALs we all know we are fundamentally alone in this life. We know this because some of us come home without a scratch, some come home in a bag or busted into pieces. We must support each other. Yet we all will be tested on our own and, most importantly, we will all face our Maker alone. That thought should stay with you every step.

—Ephraim Mattos, former Navy SEAL

If you want to survive hell, it pays to be a winner.

CHAPTER 9

DAY FOUR

If you want to survive hell, eat.

I voluntarily accept the inherent hazards of my profession, placing the welfare and security of others before my own.

—Navy SEAL Creed

Your entire body somehow aches, burns, and shivers from cold all at once as you cross the highway that divides the Naval Amphibious Base in Coronado into two sections. You are running with your boat crew, carrying your fucking boat on your heads. The SEAL instructors block civilian traffic with their vehicles; the flashing lights mounted to the vehicles split the dark, foggy morning air in brilliant pulses of white and red.

As you run across the pavement you try not to turn your head and grind the sand further into your scalp, but you strain with your eyes to look to your left and right at the northbound and southbound traffic. A handful of early morning civilian commuters sit stopped in cars and trucks blocked by the instructors' vehicles, waiting in warm, comfortable seats, watching the intersection. You can hear tunes playing, bass thumping—even this early in the predawn hours of the morning, folks like their country and hip-hop.

You peer past the windshields, catching glimpses of wide eyes gawking out at you, drivers staring in disbelief as your boat crew crosses the highway like a team of zombies in military uniforms, pinned under the weight of the rubber boats that grind away at the tops of your skulls like coarse sandpaper. Your class must look like a horror movie to the civilians stuck in their cars, like undead soldiers staggering out of the gloom, carrying one boat after another, spurred on by maniacal instructors. You can see a twentysomething girl who, if you're honest, is pretty hot holding a steaming mug in her hand while mouthing the words *What the fuck* as you pass in front of her Escalade. God, you wish you could be in her SUV, even for five minutes, to crank the heat, drink her coffee, and close your eyes. The reality of our training to the outside world makes you pause and think, *These people must really believe we are crazy to put ourselves through this.* You dismiss the thought aimlessly. *They are right: We are crazy.*

"Hurry up!" The instructors bring you back to hell. "We don't have all day!"

Your boat crew picks up the pace and it feels like a whip cracking onto your back as you hustle to keep up with the boat in front of the line. Running east, you notice a light blue and purple haze gently easing up and over the dark horizon. *Sunrise.*

Thank God, you made it to day four.

They say that if you see sunlight on Wednesday morning, you'll make it through Hell Week. There, you have seen it. The morning light. You want to bask in it. You want to be frozen in it, like a mosquito in amber.

You hope there is truth in the statement; however, you are long past relying on hope for anything. By Wednesday morning, you've fully embraced the suck. You are prepared for everything to be horrible. And you have mentally and physically gone too far into hell to quit. Quitting, in fact, is beyond inconceivable. It's not just that you do not want to do this training again, but there is *quite literally* nothing the SEAL instructors can do to you at this point to make you quit. Nothing.

As one SEAL officer says, "In Hell Week, if they had given any one of us a gun and told us to shoot ourselves in the foot, every single one of us would have done it without hesitating." In fact, shooting yourself in the foot sounds like a relatively easy task right now. You wish the instructors would propose something like shooting yourself in the foot to prove that you won't quit. *Gimme that fuckin' gun,* you would say.

But real life is not that easy, and shooting oneself in the foot would not prove something meaningful. Anyone who's a little crazy and wants something bad enough can shoot himself in the foot. What you are doing now is far, far harder. The torturous grind of Hell Week carries on and the SEAL instructors show no signs of letting up, just because they know you won't quit. In fact, it's quite the opposite. Now that they know you and your classmates won't quit, it's like they are just trying to see if they can break you.

As the sun rises on day four, the instructors lead the remaining groups in the class around the naval base for an hour. Naturally, the boats ride up high on your heads during this time while a seemingly never-ending cycle of drag races, push-ups, and degrading insults repeats itself over and over and over until at long last your class is directed to stop at the dining facility, affectionately dubbed the "chow hall."

The sun is up over the horizon and looks like a giant searchlight trying to cut through the heavy morning fog that hangs in the air over Coronado. You line up your boats in the parking lot and await your next orders. Every six hours in Hell Week you receive some kind of food. The food is not meant as a chance to get a break or for comfort, it is meant as fuel only. During Hell Week, trainees on average burn 10,000 calories but can burn up to 15,000 calories a day, equal to twenty-six and a half Big Macs, 107 twelve-ounce Cokes, or nearly four and a half cases of Bud Light. It is impossible to eat enough during Hell Week. Your body consumes fuel at an amazing rate in order to perform the physical tasks, as well as to fight off the cold and hypothermia—which is a constant.

So far, the fuel you have consumed has taken the form of cold military rations, eaten while sitting in the ocean as the surf rushes around your legs or in the wet sand next to your boats. But judging by your location, you believe you'll be eating breakfast in the chow hall.

You recall the Discovery Channel documentary *Navy SEALs Training: BUD/s Class 234*, about class 234's time during BUD/S. In the documentary, they show the meals served in the chow hall during Hell Week—trainees help themselves to a buffet of waffles, eggs, hot chocolate, orange juice, and even glorious donuts. Needless to say, you are excited to get your first hot meal since Hell Week began. Thankfully, for the first time since the week before Hell Week, your stomach feels relatively normal. A healthy and ravenous hunger has replaced what for days had been a gnawing, sick feeling in your gut. You can't wait to fill it.

As boat crews are released, you wash your hands and face and get in line headed into the chow hall.

As your crew moves toward the door, you notice another line of sailors forming to enter on the other side of the chow hall, just a few feet away. These guys are the class behind you, just beginning BUD/S and a few weeks away from Hell Week. The newbies try to ignore you. They do not want to draw the ire of the SEAL instructors, who surround you like prison bulls. And you and your class certainly don't want to draw any more unwanted attention from your tormentors. But you can't help it. You shoot glances at the next class while they stare back at you. The groups are just a few feet from each other and yet you are in entirely different worlds.

Many of these kids no doubt wish they were in your shoes,

having made it all the way to Wednesday of Hell Week, while you look at them in wonder because they are clean, soft, and scared. You are looking into a time machine at yourself just a few weeks ago, when you thought you knew what preparation and pain and sickness were. There are now two of you: who you are now, and who you were then. You are looking into your former life. Though it seems like you will never be clean, dry, or pain-free again, at some point you will take a shower and put on a spotless dry uniform without wincing like you used to. And yet you will never go back to the way you were. You will never be one of these boys again. You have spent too much time in hell. Some of the guys look scared, some look cocky and overconfident. All have no fucking clue.

As you enter the chow hall you see a small section of tables set aside for your class in the corner of the hall, as far away as possible from the main eating area where dozens of sailors eat and talk happily, like they're back in middle school lunchroom. In your corner of the chow hall, there is a pool of dead silence; men have their heads down, shoveling food into their faces. Instructors pace back and forth staring at the Hell Week trainees as if daring someone to talk. One of your classmates is caught sneaking a glance toward the other side of the chow hall and immediately receives a screaming tirade from two of the SEAL instructors. "Keep your eyes down and shut the fuck up!" This yelling causes the other side of the hall to go momentarily silent. The happy diners on the far side gawk.

You grab a plate and step up to the buffet salivating, your

mind already devouring the meal from the documentary. You can taste orange juice washing down waffles and fresh fluffy eggs. But instead of finding the fantasy meal, you see metal tubs of plain white rice, powdered eggs, and egg-battered pieces of bread. *What the fuck is this?* you think—another trick. Where is the meal from the Discovery documentary? Where are your waffles?

These thoughts come quickly and go almost as fast, as you are suddenly overwhelmed with gratitude to simply have a hot meal. A hot plate of steaming shit would be preferable to cold military rations served while standing in seawater laced with VGE.

Much later when you reflect on this meal and how it differs from what you saw in the TV documentary, you realize that you are going through SEAL training in the post-9/11 world as opposed to the guys from BUD/S class 234 who went through before 9/11. Pre-9/11 just a handful of SEAL instructors had seen any combat, going back to the '80s and '90s. Now every single one of your instructors has done multiple combat deployments to the Middle East, where they have gone kinetic with the enemy, slinging lead back and forth, taking souls. You are reminded that the United States has been at war constantly for nearly twenty years since September 11, 2001. Many of your instructors were wounded in battle, some severely. All have lost friends and fellow SEALs, and, with the rare exception of trainers who are on their last assignment, all of the men instructing you could one day be fighting overseas with you at their sides. Their business is war, and business is good. Thus there will be no sympathy from instructors tasked with weeding out the weak and preparing those who persevere for war among the ranks of the SEAL Teams. Your instructors are discovering who among your class will be the man who fights by their side, potentially saving their life one day. They are part of the careful selection process of finding the men they can count on. Eggs and bacon and a really nice meal on Wednesday morning of Hell Week doesn't mean shit to these men anymore. It is just fuel for the machine, and you are the machine.

You sit down at a table with your boat crew. Before you is a pile of bland but warm food, two cups of water, and a group of guys who will likely become your teammates. To look around at your classmates, you wouldn't know that they have just reached a huge milestone in one of the biggest trials of their lives. You see hands shaking, swollen eyes, heads nodding as everyone fights off sheer exhaustion. You see Marcos say a prayer over his plate and dig in. Your own hands still tremble from last night's long, dark, cold existence. You sit quietly, piling warm food into your mouth and swallowing. To congratulate each other, you all half-smile at each other, nod, and wink. The food you eat together seems to revive the whole team. Men who had been zombies with frozen looks of pain on their faces just hours before now can smile and look happy even. "Day four," you hear Marcos whisper from across the table. "Boys, we made it to day four."

"FEET!" an instructor shouts, making everyone jump. It's Joker. *Where the fuck did he come from?* you think.

You and your crew push back from the table and rise to attention, cheeks still filled with food.

"You fuckers think this is over!? It's only Wednesday! It's only going to get worse from here!" Joker paces behind your table. "Stop winking and nodding and smiling like a bunch of assholes. You haven't done shit." He pauses to let his words sink in. "It's only Wednesday morning, assholes. Not all of you are going to make it to Friday. Mark my words. Now, think about that while you stuff your fat faces and grin and smirk at each other."

You glance at Marcos. The crazy bastard actually winks at you and grins. Joker does not see.

You sit down and gleefully continue to stuff your *fat face*. You are uncertain how much weight you have lost, possibly twenty pounds due to the sickness, beatdown, and hypothermia. With every bland bite you feel a little better, gain a little more energy, feel your body getting what it needs. And for once in the past four days, you are having a great morning, all things considered. It won't last, that's for sure, but with a little bit of warm food inside you, you revive and are a bit more ready for whatever comes next. You have personally weathered the worst part of the storm, and you know it. The vomiting and diarrhea have slowed, and you are able to actually keep food in your body long enough for it to replenish you. There is light, but you cannot get complacent. For while there may be a brief respite from the storm, you are far from port and the end of this journey through hell.

Lesson:

Difficult times will drain us in mind, body, and spirit, and if we are to survive, we must nourish ourselves. The 15,000 calories a day that a trainee will burn during Hell Week is an extreme and obvious example of how a body is depleted, and it is also an extreme and obvious example of what it needs to keep going— food. If a trainee does not feed himself, he will not be able to complete Hell Week. This is very simple to understand. Every time an aspiring SEAL swallows some calories during this ordeal, he's putting gas in the tank of the car that will get him to the other side of hell.

In life, the same principle applies, but what we need is not as obvious as what we are using up. After all, food is rarely exactly what we need. In my own life, I gained twenty pounds during my second divorce. I certainly didn't need more calories. What I lost and needed was a sense of family and God, and I temporarily replaced those elements with junk food and booze.

It is so vital that we become aware of what we are losing during the difficult periods of our lives. If we can get precise and understand what we need, like the SEALs know the calories they require to make it through a day, we can seek out the right elements to feed ourselves.

What is more, when we are in our own hell, we do not have instructors with us ensuring we take care of our bodies by force-feeding us every six hours. Instead, we have friends, family, and spiritual leaders who guide us, or, in the case of many, we have false friends and leaders who misguide us. Just like with what we put in our bodies and into our souls, we need to make sure the people closest to us, our "instructors" who intentionally or unintentionally inform our lives, are the kinds of people who will give us what we need. As much as trainees in Hell Week may suffer under their trainers, they know and trust them to provide the right food for the task. We too must find those proven people, cut out the bad ones, and then help the good family, friends, and spiritual leaders to understand what we need as we trust that they will help guide us to it.

It's really simple. You need to be tough to be a SEAL. You need to be smart if you want to stay in the game, and this means taking care of yourself. You're a fucking asshole and a fool if you disrespect your body. Eat, motherfucker.

—DZ, former Navy SEAL

If you want to survive hell, eat.

CHAPTER 10

DAY FOUR

If you want to survive hell, become a better brother.

"Two minutes!" an instructor yells inside the chow hall. "If you're already done, get a swim buddy and go stand by the boats outside! We have more games to play."

Just like that, you are tossed back into the fray of Hell Week. You push back from your table, return your tray and drag your ass out of the chow hall, pick up the boat, put it on your head, and carry it around the base and beach for a couple miles.

You are rapidly approaching the ninety-six-hour mark—though your mind cannot do the math, you know you have almost completed a total of four straight days without sleep, piled on top of a sickened and malnourished body and mind. Up until this point in the training every moment has been palpably painful, everything has hurt, and you felt it all. Each jarring time the boat landed on your head it registered with you like a drumbeat in a song you have memorized. That is how it seems until the blurring effect eventually takes over your brain. Now the peaks of pain blur with the valleys, and each moment seems like the last. It's as if you are drowning in pain, your vision shrinks, and you are looking out of a small porthole of a sinking ship. You gasp for each breath of air and look out the window and can only see what is immediately in front of you—the spot where you put each foot in front of the other in the sinking sand. You lose your sense of time, and time loses all sense of meaning. The difference between fifteen seconds and one hour is meaningless, because there is no end to the suffering. The moment of pain just lasts forever, going on and on. You are delirious, sick, and malnourished, you are knocking on the door of total exhaustion, and you don't mean "flop on the couch exhaustion," you mean collapse into the dirt because your brain and body shut down entirely. After ninety-six hours straight with no sleep, the human brain starts to break down in irreversible ways. You know it has to stop—even for a short period of time—but it doesn't. This is the furthest the SEAL instructors can push students without literally starting to kill them.

Joker's threat that not everyone would make through Hell Week sadly comes true when your class stops for its daily medical check. A handful of students have developed fractures in their legs from running more than 150 miles under forty or fifty pounds of extra weight from the boats and rucks. Like racing ponies put out to pasture, those guys are done for now.

Others are literally drowning from the fluid building up in their lungs. Their pneumonia has overtaken their lungs. They cannot breathe sufficiently and are put on oxygen and antibiotics and given IVs. They, too, are done. And they are pissed. One pneumonic classmate is so pissed and determined to be back in training that he yanks the oxygen tubes from his nose and tries to rush past the medics, but he is too weak, and is given a Xanax and a promise that he will have another shot. Some really unlucky bastards have developed life-threatening oozing sores from the open chafing wounds that plague the entire class. They look like they have leprosy—their skin sloughing off, oozing pus and smelling like death.

All of these men are pulled from training. They will be given the option to return to selection in two months' time after they recuperate; however, if they choose to return to training, they will be required to start BUD/S from the beginning. If they want to be SEALs, they will have to suffer through all this shit over again, including four days of Hell Week—not because they quit, but because their bodies simply broke. You do not want to be one of these poor bastards. But if your body, God forbid, breaks, you will do it all over again. You want it bad enough. And most of these men do too. Some, however, will likely take the chance to use the medical out as a reason to stop trying to become a SEAL again, which of course is the same thing as quitting. It only sounds like you're less of a pussy.

After the medical check, you dress once again in a clean

wet uniform and promptly follow the instruction to "go get wet and sandy, you sacks of shit!" You turn yourself into a sugar cookie and then, having to use the bathroom but never having a break, you just piss yourself in the sand. It feels good until the hot acidic urine reaches the raw flesh-free zone between your legs and it's as if someone poured hydrochloric acid onto your balls.

More painful brain blur occurs as the mind- and body-decimating punishment of Hell Week continues and lasts into early afternoon. Finally, you have hit the ninety-five-hour mark and you are to receive your first rest of Hell Week. "Everyone head to the tents on the beach," an instructor yells. "Nighty-night time."

You are about to take the infamous two-hour nap.

The instructors order your class to file into the same green military tents in which you started this terrible ordeal four days earlier. Those simple tents where you sat huddled in cold darkness awaiting the beginning of Hell Week are now a welcome refuge. They are dry and warmed by the late afternoon sun. The fabric flutters from a gentle ocean breeze that toys with the flaps of the tent.

"Hurry up! Hurry up!" the SEAL instructors harass you as you file in.

Inside each of the tents are two rows of green cots, their feet stuck into the sand. It's like a dream. A luxury beach suite in Polynesia could not possibly be more welcoming. Nothing in your life has ever seemed more beautiful and serene. You walk over to a cot and stand next to it, staring at it like it's a king-sized featherbed. You'd dive into it right now if you could. But you have to wait for the rest of your classmates to come in.

Just days before, your class had barely been able to fit into these tents. Now the inside is spacious, with more than enough room for all of you. You have been so caught up in your own misery and trying to live through the never-ending cycle of beatdowns that you didn't even realize you had lost half of your class. Twice as many men, all young soldiers in the prime of their lives and in peak physical condition, had crowded into these same tents four days earlier. Shit had gotten very hard over the past ninety-six hours, and at some point, a full half of your class—a group of men who had already hung on and survived the first major purging during the initial three weeks of BUD/S—had either given up and quit or been rolled back to the next class because of sickness or injury. Only about 50 of you remained. The other 150 men who came to Coronado are now somewhere outside of the tent, warm, dry, well fed, and rested. And without a doubt, those 150 men are also filled with crushing regret and self-loathing, which they will likely carry with them for the rest of their lives. You don't pity the quitters. They chose to succumb to weakness. And you don't pity the men who were injured. They don't want your fucking pity, they want to be SEALs. They want to be with you. And you know they will have their chance to endure this shit again.

You now turn your entire focus to the men who remain

with you, the men who stand with you in the tent, shivering, bent, broken, and chafed raw. The uncommitted, the weak, the broken have been purged by the selection process. Everyone in that tent has proved, beyond a doubt, that they are committed to doing whatever it takes to become a SEAL. But commitment only goes so far. You still have the rest of Wednesday and then all of Thursday and Friday to go without breaking. And no longer is quitting a fear. No one will quit from here on out. Now the struggle is about survival. The fight is about making it to the end. Even though three-quarters of the men who started this program with you are gone, you, for the first time, are not alone.

The dynamics have changed. You are no longer a lone man trying to survive. You now stand with these men who remain, and you know they are your true brothers and you would do anything for them, and they would do anything for you. You will complete this training not alone, but as a team. Or you will not complete it at all.

The last student enters the tent. "Lay down!" an instructor screams. "We'll be back in two hours, and you are going to suffer. If you know what's good for you, you'll do yourself a favor and never wake up. You'll just sleep in and stay in that cot."

The SEAL instructors exit the tent, leaving only trainees inside. Outside the tent, a team of corpsmen—medics—and BUD/S students from the class ahead of yours, who have already completed Hell Week, stand just outside the doors, just in case a medical emergency presents itself. Believe it or not, taking this fucking nap is one of the hardest things you'll ever attempt to do in your life.

You want to drop onto the cot, but that would be far too painful. And you cannot move quickly. You slowly lower yourself down onto the thin fabric covering the cot. You are in serious pain; your lower back and hip have seized and are scarcely able to move. You know your back is badly injured (in fact, you will learn that you have a ruptured disk in your spine and several cracked ribs), and you suspect your hip is partially dislocated (it is), but you won't see a doctor so you can't do anything meaningful about the pain you are experiencing. All you can do is try to sleep. Which you try to do. You squeeze your eyes shut and ball up on your side. Unfortunately, you quickly realize your mind and body simply will not shut down. Precious sleep, even just two hours of it, isn't going to happen for you. You hover in a state of wakefulness with moments of unconsciousness—it's a bit like trying to look into a yard through slats in a fence as you ride along the fence on a bike. You can see in flashes of sight into the backyard, yet every half second your view is blocked.

You curl into a fetal position, and your wet and sandy uniform sticks to your body. You stare at the man on the cot next to you. The dude on it is Marcos. He snores and twitches and shakes as his body goes into overdrive trying to repair the damage. His swollen eyes dart back and forth behind his eyelids as he lies in an unconscious heap, oblivious to the world around him. You envy him, but you do not envy his inevitable wake-up. That will suck.

In his dreams, you imagine he may have been dreaming of Christmas, which is right around the corner, with his family. You bet that in Marcos's dream it's warm and cozy inside by the fire, booze-free eggnog is served in small crystal glasses, cookies are set out on a plate, his mom is knitting a sweater, his dad is singing hymns, and outside the wind howls across an Ohio field and piles snow up on the windowsill. It's good to be inside where it's warm by the fire. You pity what will happen to Marcos and his sweet sugarplum dreams when instructors return and he's dragged back into your all-too-real nightmare.

Near the entrance of the tent, two students lie huddled together in the sand underneath the beams of sunlight that filter in through the flaps and holes in the tent. One of the men convulses as he dry-heaves. You can hear his teeth jack-hammering each other. It sounds like a woodpecker, the hammering noises only interrupted by epileptic-like convulsions, groaning and whimpering. The sailor must have contracted VGE during Hell Week. The other man lies behind him, arms wrapped around the sick man to try to keep him warm, so his buddy will not be rolled back. The man helping his buddy out is not worried about the stench, or the filth, or the awkwardness of basically spooning a dude, or the very real risk of getting sick and damaging his own chances of completion. He risks it all to help his brother. This is where and how the true bonds of the SEALs are formed. Later, when each of these men is in battle, he will need to protect his brother SEAL in combat, risking his own life to protect the SEAL next to him. A bond of brotherhood that fire and death and destruction cannot break is forged in moments like these.

The two hours pass by, simultaneously excruciatingly slow and yet somehow instant. Time makes no sense to you anymore. You are in and out of consciousness. And though you are not sleeping, you are resting and slowing down and you can feel you are almost about to fall into a deep and wonderful sleep when you hear the shuffle of feet and muffled angry voices outside the tent. You curl up into a fetal position, staring at Marcos across from you. *This can't be fucking real. The instructors can't be back this soon.*

Without warning, the high-pitched wail of several sirens cuts through the thin fabric of the tent and shatters your brain into a million tiny shards. All peace is destroyed.

"HIT THE SURF!" the instructors scream, more belligerently than usual. "HIT THE FUCKING SURF!"

You try to get up, but your body has gone completely rigid, your muscles have locked into place. Instead of getting to your feet, you let out an involuntary gasp of pain. "Ahhhhhhhh!" You can't help it, you literally scream like a girl. Similar gasps and screams of shock and pain fill that tent. The sound is witchy, like a fucking haunted house that has been lit on fire. In a surreal moment of near mass hysteria, almost every other man is experiencing the same phenomenon—their bodies, having been given two hours to rest, have in fact become locked into place, like corpses stiffened by rigor mortis. Each man is seized by excessive lactic acid buildup in his muscles. Each man's body is twisted and crippled. It is only by force of will alone that you are able to start moving. "Fuuuuuuuuucccccccckkkkk!" you yell as you push your body into a seated position. You are out of breath, huffing for oxygen and shaking like you just lifted a five-thousand-pound car off a baby. You see others moving, screaming. It's only been ten seconds or so, but you can hear the officers yelling, getting more pissed, making more threats. You are trying to get your legs to straighten out. You feel like you need to beat them. You hear intense guttural moaning and look to see Marcos paralyzed in pain on his cot. He looks terrified; you can't tell if he's still in his dream or not. You limp over to him and shake him awake. "Bro, we need to go!"

His eyes finally roll open. His eyes blink, unseeing and unfocused. Then the eyes snap into focus and look to you, pleading for help. "Come on, buddy, get up!"

You pull him out of his cot as he starts to scream. You don't understand a word, but you see his legs straighten, and suddenly he is on his feet and moving.

Joker ducks into the tent. "Hurry the fuck up, you goddamn turds!" His megaphone's siren fills the small space with ear-splitting noise, making you wince. The class staggers zombie-like out of the tents and to the beach, the walking dead.

"Oh, you're all fucked now!" Joker then makes a weird exaggerated laughing sound. "Muah-ha-ha-ha!" He continues to taunt the class with this villainous laugh as you approach the berm. Your back is spasming, your legs are giving out, you no longer have the capacity to bend at the waist, and you nearly fall backward as you start up the steep, sandy embankment. You reach down and try to drag your left leg along with you.

As a class, you pour over the berm, everyone running like their limbs are not their own. You make it to the flat beach to now stride out in a full-frontal assault against the frigid waves. You feel like you're in a reverse D-Day landing—running into the water to get killed. You glance to your side at Marcos running next to you, and see tears streaming down his face in uncontrolled streams. His lips curl in misery, and his eyes are swollen yet locked in defiance. They look out in a murderous stare at the wintry Pacific Ocean. His face is slick with tears, but he never falters or wavers. Marcos plunges straight into the ocean beside you.

The shock of cold water stings every micrometer of your body. The salty wave cascades over your head, pummels your body, and engulfs your senses. You force yourself to your feet as your body buckles in pain from the shock of the cold water. When this shock wears off, the pain is replaced by saltwater burning your freshly open wounds. Scabs tear away as the sand and water chafe away between your legs, under your armpits, around your beltline, and around your neck.

Fuccckkkkkkk this hurts. You want to scream, but you don't. You just part run, part hobble back to the berm.

"Get sandy!" Joker commands. "Become a sugar cookie, now."

You drop facedown, roll and nuzzle in the sand, and grab handfuls of sand and pat it so it covers literally every inch of your body—head, neck, hair, face, every part of your uniform, ears, eyes, lips, nose. This sucks so bad. And it is getting so much harder to embrace the suck.

In the midst of your collective misery, a cry of defiance rings out from one of the students. "Hooyah!" he yells. Another man joins in, and then another. You join in as well: "Hooyah!"

You scream as you and your crew frantically cover yourselves in sand.

"Shut up! Shut the fuck up!" Joker screams back at you.

The screaming of "Hooyah!" doesn't let up.

"Drop, you motherfuckers! I'll fucking teach you!" Joker yells, trying to regain control and, naturally, break your spirits like he's kicking in a headlight. But you are not that fragile.

You drop facedown in the sand and do twenty push-ups as a class, counting out each of the reps. This stops the cries of "Hooyah!" For now . . .

You remain in the push-up, aka "leaning rest," position, while Joker and the other instructors pace around your class.

"You fucking turds love to run your mouths, don't you?" Joker says. "Well, how about you follow fucking orders instead? When we tell you to shut up, just shut the fuck up!"

"Hooyah," a random student mutters under his breath.

"Who said that!?" an instructor says. "Tell me now, or you will all pay."

No one says a word.

"Roger that," Joker says. "Everyone on your feet."

You stand at attention as the SEAL walks through your jumbled ranks. "Everyone get a handful of sand and put it in your mouth. Now," Joker says calmly.

You pick up a handful of soggy sand and put it in your mouth. The sand grinds against your teeth as you struggle to breathe through your stuffed-up nose.

"That's better," the SEAL says. "Now spit it out and hit the surf!"

You spit the sand from your mouth and head once again back to the cold ocean.

As you emerge from the water, the SEALs order you to link arms and walk back into the ocean as a class to be surf tortured. With arms locked, you sit in the ocean as wave after wave of salty, sandy, frigid water crashes over your bodies, filling your eyes, ears, and noses with water. Your bodies burn, lips turn blue, and limbs shake uncontrollably as mild hypothermia sets in.

"Hooyah!" a student yells through chattering lips.

"Hooyah!" As a class you return the call with one defiant voice, giving the SEAL instructors a proverbial collective middle finger and showing them that you may be beaten down but that they have not broken your spirit.

The SEAL instructors remain silent as they stand shin deep in the water looking down at you as you freeze. You are brothers, locked in arms, defiant and fighting for your lives. This is exactly the mindset the instructors want from you.

Lesson:

It is all too easy to become so centered on our own pain and struggles in life that we forget others are going through hard times. But when we take a step back and see how we can help others we find not only purpose, but also lifelong friends.

If you can get a group of people to work together relentlessly and selflessly toward a common goal where a person would rather die than let down a teammate, that group will always be a greater force to be reckoned with. There must be a point of no return where you commit all to accomplish the goal. When you reach that point you are unbeatable.

If you want to survive hell, fight alongside your true brothers, not against them.

You will complete this training not alone, but as a team. Or you will not complete it at all.

There is a phenomenon with the SEALs that I have witnessed time and time again. It really doesn't matter how badly you fuck up, as long as you fuck *somebody else* up. In other words, when a SEAL does something really bad—say, for example, literally kills somebody—that does not automatically cause expulsion from the team. As long as the person killed was not a team guy, or family of a team guy.

Witness, for example, the case of Eddie Gallagher. Eddie was accused of killing an injured ISIS member who was in the custody of coalition forces. Not exactly Geneva Convention compliant—but the SEALs couldn't really have cared less. In fact, one of his teammates (a medic) ended up taking responsibility for the death, after he was given immunity from prosecution by the Navy. Arguably this was somewhat of a predictable event.

While I was not there, and can only speculate on the exact discussion, I can envision the consultation with the lawyer leading up to the testimony of the SEAL who was given immunity.

> **SEAL**: Let me see if I understand this: I can say whatever I want, and take responsibility for anything up to and including having a part in the death of this ISIS member, and cannot be prosecuted for the act?
> **Lawyer**: Yes, that is correct.
> **SEAL**: Okay, I did it. I finished him.

When this graphic and life-changing testimony was released from the trial, I was neither shocked nor even amazed. It was essentially code. One teammate had the opportunity to cover his buddy's back (six), and he did it. Was the testimony given true? I don't know that either, but it really did not matter in SEAL terms. It was effective in eliminating the threat then existing on another teammate whom you were in battle next to. The more interesting dynamic is that even though Big Navy elected to prosecute Gallagher, even though the case was suspect from day one, they failed to understand the dynamic of the SEALs/Hell Week mentality.

Loyalty and brotherhood are values we should cherish and strive toward. Instead, loyalty and brotherhood in modern times, and in the media, have become buzzwords for proving bad behavior, covering up and excusing mistakes. In this world we live in of "me too" takedowns that occur decades after a supposed event, executives can never know who will tear them down, and the perception is that anyone who wants to see loyalty is looking for an excuse. First, expecting loyalty from your teammate—even if that means publicly covering up mistakes—is not altogether a bad thing. The reality is we need to be able to make mistakes and improve. Also, brothers who are loyal to each other do not let them make mistakes. SEALs who see fellow SEALs failing to live up to the standards of the trident step in and work with their brother to bring him up to the mark.

In civilian life, successful teamwork is based on trust. There CANNOT be a successful team without trust. You don't have to like, admire, or even respect your teammates to accomplish a mission, but you have to be able to rely on them to do their part in the mission—that is trust. Loyalty, support, helping to take your teammates up to a higher level is what good brothers (and sisters) do—these are extensions built upon the basis of trust. The way to win trust and win more missions is to become more trustworthy, more loyal, more supportive in the face of disaster, more sacrificing—these are the qualities that will make you a better person, a better leader, a better teammate, and a better brother and will lift you out of the hardest times and propel you toward success in any theater.

Monday morning quarterbacking seems to be a cottage industry in our modern world. "He should have thrown this pass." "She should have made this objection during trial." Blah, blah, blah. Perhaps Teddy Roosevelt said it best:

> It is not the critic who counts; not the man who points out how the strong man stumbles, or where the doer of deeds could have done them better. The credit belongs to the man who is actually in the arena, whose face is marred by dust and sweat and blood; who strives valiantly; who errs, who comes short again and again, because there is no effort without error and shortcoming; but who does actually strive to do the deeds; who knows great enthusiasms, the great devotions; who spends himself in a worthy cause; who at the best knows in the end the triumph of high achievement, and who at the worst, if he fails, at least fails while daring greatly, so that his place shall never be with those cold and timid souls who neither know victory nor defeat.

This is why I have made it my life's passion to help men and women of the military in need—particularly SEALs. Perhaps that is why they trust me. I honor those who have stepped up and made the sacrifice to get in the arena for our country. I don't second-guess the reasons for their actions in combat. I was not there; I did not see or go through the hell they did.

But I am keenly aware that they went through that hell for you and me to live a better life with our families and children here. For that reason, I never second-guess decisions made on a battlefield. As an American I believe I owe this to our brothers and sisters, sons and daughters who made the decision to serve. We have seen more men and women prosecuted for war crimes in the last twenty years than in the entirety of U.S. history, all wars. And this is bullshit. It is a reflection of those who served being second-guessed by those who have never set foot on the field of battle, aka the arena. "Rules of engagement" have been used to prosecute those who would not let a brother die, even if it meant a court-martial for his acts. This does not bode well for our country, or those who would give their lives in defense of its Constitution. That is why I defend them to a fault.

I believe the same respect and support should be given to the men and women who are in law enforcement here in the United States. It has become all too in vogue for people to run down the police for alleged brutality, racial animus, and related criticisms. The majority of the cases that have been alleged to be examples of "bad behavior" by the police in fact are not evidence of anything but the half-cocked press trying to inflame the populace for their own political positions. The reality is that our police are many times placed into positions every bit as dangerous and kinetic as our warfighting community. One must seriously consider what this does for the ability of the military and the police to recruit our finest in the future. Who wants to do the job with the knowledge that there is a very real possibility you could be prosecuted for it?

The bottom line is that the politicians and the press second-guessing every use of force by our military and our police degrades their readiness to do the job they were hired to do, that is, take out the bad guys.

If you want to survive hell, become a better brother.

PART IV

THE END IS A MIRAGE

CHAPTER 11

DAY FIVE

If you want to survive hell, NEVER half-ass anything.

In the worst of conditions, the legacy of my teammates steadies my resolve and silently guides my every deed.

—Navy SEAL Creed

Dawn breaks on Thursday morning after a cold, miserable night of surf torture, an untold number of push-ups, and more than ten miles of running while carrying a fucking boat on top of your head. By now, your body is not just tired, it is beginning to truly break down. You think you're running at an all-out sprint but your speed is only a quick jog, and you can only complete push-ups by straightening your arms, lifting your hips and knees off the ground, then collapsing back to the sand as if you were humping it. And then, of course, you have to begin another repetition of the same, over and over and over.

Despite the seeming chaos that is Hell Week, you know the

entire event is a carefully choreographed dance. Every mile is logged, every evolution is calculated, and every surf torture is timed down to the minute. SEAL instructors, accompanied by Navy corpsmen medical support teams, monitor the class constantly for sickness, injury, and hypothermia. This level of care is taken partly to ensure that no one dies, but also to ensure that the instructors are free to push you and your class to the limits of what humans can endure—scientific torture, with men standing by to keep you alive. With every variable accounted for, the SEAL instructors are able to bring down the hammer as hard as possible and yet stop a razor breadth short of killing you. The accumulated pain and misery experienced are impossible to put into words. By the end of the week, you are no longer able to form words, let alone shape your own thoughts, and as you will soon experience, you will actually begin to lose your fucking mind and start seeing some strange shit. And yet you have to go all out and stay 100 percent focused on the task at hand.

"It's only Wednesday, boyos," Joker says as he paces between the students lying in the cold surf attempting to hump sand.

If your heart could flop out of your chest and bury itself like a clam into the lump of wet sand you are dry humping, it would. And you wouldn't care. You are devastated. You thought it was Thursday. Isn't it Thursday? You try to count the nights. You try to remember what day you are on, but you can't.

You hear Marcos say, "Sir, wait, isn't it Thursday?"

"You turds still have two more days of this. I wouldn't lie to you," he says matter-of-factly. "Trust me, it's Wednesday."

It can't actually be Wednesday, you think. *Could it?* Another day seems like an impossibility.

You look over at the man to your right, fucking his pile of sand or supposedly doing push-ups. "Dude," you whisper, "it's Wednesday?" Seeing the quizzical look on your face, he rolls his eyes and shakes his head. Then he glowers up at Joker, who's got a huge grin on his face, and is whistling and singing the song "Zip-a-Dee-Doo-Dah."

Zip-a-dee-doo-dah, zip-a-dee-ay,
My, oh my, what a wonderful day.

Motherfucker.

At this point in Hell Week, your mind starts to play tricks on you. The concept of time is irrelevant. Numbers, distances, and days of the week are all the same. The only thing that's real is the present moment and the pain you feel. You have no idea if the instructor is telling the truth or not, and it does not matter. All you know is his job is to make you ring the ever-present bell three times.

What a sadistic asshole, you think as you finish your push-ups and, soaked to the core, stand at ragged attention next to your classmates, shivering uncontrollably and covered in sand. You and your class form a line, standing on the beach in a row of boats facing the ocean.

"Rig for sea!" an instructor yells into the megaphone.

As a crew, you stow your covers in your pockets and then reach into your boat to grab life jackets and helmets, all while the instructors yell and, using wooden oars, fling scoops of sand at you, aiming for faces, mouths, and eyes.

"Hurry up! Hurry up! You have ten seconds!" the instructor with the megaphone shouts.

As expected, the crew doesn't make the unrealistic timeline and is punished for the failure with more push-ups—this time you must do the dry humping with your feet elevated on the side of the boat. Needless to say, you can't do your push-ups correctly and so are awarded two more sets of push-ups.

Finally, ready to go to sea, you stand beside your boats facing the Pacific Ocean. Plunging waves obscure the horizon. The surf is big today, bigger than usual. The waves seem to build into a constantly forming wall that crashes down with a loud clap, a blast of white foam, and a thundering roar. You feel like Sisyphus—your boat is your boulder, the line of surf is your mountain. You all know what is coming next.

"Okay, boyos. This is a race," Joker begins. "Paddle out past the surf zone, dump boat, and then paddle back to shore. The first team back gets to sit out the next race. It pays to be a winner. Go!"

Your team picks up the boat by its handles and rushes to the surf zone. Your legs pump and push against the incoming waves as you haul the fucking boat out to waist-deep water. The two men at the front of the boat jump in first, followed by the men on either side of the middle of the boat, and then the last three men jump in. The boat crew leader sits in the back middle using his paddle as a rudder and calling cadence.

As a team, you paddle ferociously to the cadence called by the boat crew leader, struggling to keep the bow of the boat facing directly into the waves. To your right, a boat crew doesn't keep their boat straight enough and a wave picks up their boat and dumps it on its side, sending the entire crew flailing into the ocean.

"Water!" your front men yell, indicating that a wave is about to hit us. (Students use the term "water" because "wave" sounds too much like "wait.") A wave picks up the bow of your boat and lifts it up in the air. You bend forward, using your weight to carry it over to the other side, and continue paddling.

A wall of water suddenly two to three times bigger than the already huge surf rises from the ocean, obscuring any signs of the horizon—this is a rogue wave. The wall towers five feet above your heads and only grows larger. Without being told, you paddle as hard as you can to get ahead of the water, but it is too late.

The bow of your boat shoots straight into the air as the wall of water reaches it. The first two men are thrown over your head into the cold ocean. Moments later, you too are picked up and thrown.

The world goes black as you plunge into the ocean and are swallowed by the massive wall of water. The shock of cold water sends chills through your already mildly hypothermic body as you struggle to hold on to your paddle. Pulled by the wave, you tumble head over heels in a roaring torrent, smashing into the sandy seabed.

You pop up on the surface gasping for air, and somehow manage to stand as the water recedes, sucking back to the sea, in preparation for the next wave. Your eyes sting from the saltwater and you blink, trying to clear your vision as you look around for your boat crew. Many men in orange life jackets and overturned boats lie scattered among the surf zone. Your team is clearly not the only one that has been taken out by the rogue wave.

You help another member of your team to his feet and together wade through the surf to your overturned boat. The rest of your crew stands there already and are in fact in the process of flipping the boat back over.

"Everyone good? Still have your paddles?" your boat crew leader asks. You nod. "Roger that. Let's go!"

Again, you push your boat out toward the crashing waves and climb on board. By now, you can see that several crews have made it past the surf zone and are intentionally flipping their boats over as the race rules require. Knocked down, but definitely not knocked out of the race, you paddle frantically to avoid being caught by another massive wave and make it out past the last breakers.

As ordered, you intentionally flip your boat over in an exercise designed to dump water out of the boat while at sea. The water temperature in the 50s immediately begins to suck the energy out of your body—whatever is left in it—and you still have to wait to get out of it. Four men climb into the boat, while you and another man slip into the water and hold on to the side as the boat crew leader treads water and gives orders. On his command, the four men in the boat lean back and tip the boat over, pulling you and the other man onto the top (or bottom) of the now turned-over (i.e., upside-down) boat. You pull two more men onto the upturned boat and then, grabbing the side, flip it back over to its upright position. You scramble back onto the boat, commence paddling, and head toward shore.

Collectively the team pumps and paddles, trying to catch up to the boats ahead of yours. These lucky boat teams are already headed to shore. You will not win this event. Then, suddenly another rogue wave comes out of nowhere, picks the lead boat up by its stern, and smashes it back into the ocean, sending its crew flying. Caught in deep water, the crew of this boat tries desperately to get a man back onto the overturned boat, while your team is still afloat and getting pounded by wave after wave of freezing water. It feels as if the waves that don't flip the boat literally grab it like a large flat rock and throw it toward the shore like a skipping stone. It's like your enemy, the God of the Deep, is throwing your ass back to land.

Your team makes it to the shore without further disaster, but you find yourselves in third place. You all know what that means.

"You fucking turds clearly don't want to put out!" Joker

screams in your faces. "Taking your time out there like we have all goddamn day!"

You take the scolding as a compliment. You aren't in first place, but you have somehow managed to come in third out of eight boat crews, despite your rough start. That's a decent showing. The instructors know that, but they never want you to ever become complacent and accept anything other than total victory. Even if you win, that isn't enough. You are expected to annihilate your opponents no matter how tired or miserable you are.

"Second place is first losers," Joker scoffs in disgust to the boat crew next to you who had come in second place. "All of you drop!"

You drop into the push-up position in the sand to wait for the other crews to return. Arms quivering and backs sagging, you watch as two crews who have been tossed by the waves struggle to regroup on their boats. You can see that one of the men has lost his paddle in the surf. He will surely pay for that. Others are vomiting water and sand, trying to recover from the near-drowning experience.

"Same race!" an instructor suddenly yells before the last two crews have returned. "Go!"

You pop to your feet, pick up your boat, and shuffle as fast as you can into the ocean. You pass the scattered crews, who look at your group in dismay. They know they'll never be able to catch up to you, but they are expected to give a 110 percent effort to try to beat you.

"Water!" your front men call. Another dark green wall of water looms menacingly ahead.

"Paddle through wave!" your boat crew leader screams.

The wave picks up your bow and threatens to flip your boat, but you paddle with every remaining ounce of strength you and your team have. Leaning forward and paddling, you brace for the shock. Cold water crashes over your heads, but you keep paddling. Moments later, the calm ocean is all that you can see to the horizon and you realize you are one of only two boats that made it through the wave.

"Dump boat!" your boat crew leader screams. Like clockwork, you repeat the same process as before, flipping your rubber boat upside down and then flipping it back right side up.

As you climb back into the boat, you look over to see that the other boat crew is slightly ahead of your crew and heading to shore. This is your one and only chance to catch them and win.

Somehow finding more strength somewhere within, your team rows fast and hard. Your boat crew leader screams the cadence in excitement as you start to gain on the other crew. The leader of the crew in front of you looks back and sees that you are gaining. He barks a few orders to his crew and guides their boat directly into your path as you enter the surf zone. This is a racing move—cutting you off. And it is a dangerous one. You and the men in your boat are only partially in control of your craft. You have an all-powerful ocean bucking beneath you.

"Oh shit. What the hell is he doing!?" your boat crew leader yells. The last thing any of you want is to get stuck in a traffic jam in the surf zone. That's how people get hurt and kicked out less than forty-eight hours from the end of Hell Week. The boats are supposed to stay in their lanes to avoid this kind of thing, but knowing he is going to lose the race, the other boat crew leader decides to block your path and force you all to go down with them.

You scream insults and curse the other boat's crew (and the crew's mothers and their piece-of-shit fathers) as your bow rams into their stern. The other team's boat crew leader turns around and screams back at you, but you have no idea what he says. Suddenly, he goes silent as his eyes grow wide.

"Water!" he screams and points behind you.

A rumbling sound begins building behind the boat, as a dark shadow of a wave blots out the afternoon sun. You don't turn to look at it but instead grab your paddle with both hands and hold your breath. This is going to end very badly.

The stern of your boat is suddenly lifted vertically and sent flying ten feet in the air. Time slows down as you fly over the heads of the men in the boat crew ahead of you. You watch as if in slow motion as your boat flips upside down and lands right on top of the other boat crew, sandwiching your class-mates between the two boats. As the impact occurs—in a brief instant you see one of the crew receive a blow from the edge of your hard rubber boat right in the face. It's Marcos. He's taken a direct hit from your bow. He's wearing a helmet, but it is as if he's taken a rubber bat, swung by Neptune, right in the kisser. The sound the hit makes is horrible, like eggs cracking under a foot, but you know the eggs are your friend's nose, lips, and jaw.

You don't see what happens to him next. Your world becomes dark and cold as you plunge headfirst into the water just three feet in front of the two boats. The boats and students trapped between them hit you in the stomach before gravity can fully submerge you.

You are dragged along, like a rag doll under the water, as the boats smash and flip in the violent surf. You curl into a fetal position and force yourself to focus on one thing only: Hold on to the paddle! Loss of your paddle is treated by the instructors like the loss of your firearm—with extreme prejudice. You feel a surge of relief as your life jacket begins pulling you back to the surface. Suddenly, your back hits something solid. *Am I on the bottom of the ocean?* you think. *No, that's not possible.*

Lungs burning, you realize you are stuck underneath one of the overturned boats. Holding on to your paddle with one arm, you use the other arm to force yourself out from under the edge of the boat. You pop to the surface and gasp for air, right as another wave smashes into your face and drags you under yet again. You curl into the fetal position, still holding on to your paddle while you choke and cough under the water. Somehow you manage to relax in this sea storm, a sensation you would feel in the future when being buffeted by the forces of nature.

Finally, you feel the familiar texture of the sand in shallow water. Bracing your legs, you pop your head above the surface, seeing stars from the near loss of consciousness. You turn your face away from the waves and suck in sweet air between coughing fits.

A hand reaches out and grabs you. "You alright, man?" your boat crew leader asks.

"Yeah, I'm alive," you mutter between coughs.

"That is insane, man. That other boat crew leader is a fucking idiot. Still got your paddle?"

"Yeah."

You and the leader wade through the surf and find your scattered crew and boat, which has ended up right side up.

"We can still win!" one of our guys yells, pointing. The violent wave has carried your boat and your entire crew almost to the shore.

You and your crew grab your boat and begin pushing it to shore as another crew paddles just behind you in the shallows.

Your boat hits sand. Just a few yards away on the beach, the SEAL instructors stand motionless, arms folded, watching.

"Let's go! Let's go!" your boat crew leader screams, trying to stay ahead of the other boat, which has just hit the sand as well. "Up boat!"

Your crew bends down to pick up the boat and carry it to the finish line, but to your dismay it is filled to the brim with seawater. You can't pick it up.

"Dump boat!" everyone screams frantically as you and your crew struggle to tip the boat on its side.

Water flows out of your boat and onto the sand as the other crew lifts their boat and starts toward the instructors.

"Go! Go! Go!" You pick up your boat and race after them, but it is too late. Despite all the effort, the good luck of getting out first, the bullshit move by the crew, and the lucky wave that almost brought you back to the front of the race, you have lost.

You stand next to your boat as a SEAL instructor comes over. "Hey assholes. You shouldn't let water get into your boat."

You stand silently in defeat, as your chest heaves from exhaustion and water drips from your soaked uniform. The winning crew sits on the edge of their boat taking a coveted break.

A big grin flashes over the SEAL's face. "You guys know what second place is, right?" he asks.

"First loser," your boat crew leader replies.

"That's right. Drop!"

You drop into the push-up position in the sand to wait for the rest of the crews and the next race, when you hear whistles blowing, yelling. Corpsmen, your medics, are racing toward the surf. Something is wrong. As you look back out to sea, the boat that cut you off is being dragged by its team toward the shore. Its crew leader is signaling for help. A man is pulled from the boat, his body looking limp and lifeless. His face looks like a cherry pie that has been smashed with a baseball bat. It's Marcos. You can see blood bubbling in his nostrils, so you know he's breathing, and it appears as if he is clenching something—you can't believe it—his fucking paddle. He's not dead, hopefully no permanent neck injuries, and he's not out of the program entirely, but he's certainly going to be rolled back to the next class and have to do this all over again, all because his crew leader fucked up and tried to cheat his way ahead.

Lesson:

Despite pain and hardship, SEALs are expected to keep moving and always stay competitive. Defeat is never an option. They are expected to give 100 percent effort 100 percent of the time. The consequences of not going all out in war are obvious. You can get killed, you can get your teammates killed, and you can fail in your mission. But the truth is in life there are many ways to give up and suffer both metaphorical and real deaths. In the SEALs and in life, when a dickhead makes a bad choice—even in a closely monitored training exercise surrounded by medics—the results can be catastrophic. Worse, when we let our guards down and perform at less than 100 percent, others, innocent people, can get injured. A mechanic who rebuilds a motor with hundreds of parts but fails to tighten one bolt can set in motion events that will lead to disaster and maybe death, even dozens of deaths if, say, the lost bolt is in an engine of a 747.

We must be vigilant always—and we must have each other's backs. Even when we experience the worst and hardest times—the most hellacious shit—it becomes paramount not to become apathetic and lose our edge. Retain your edge by fighting to win and give 100 percent, even in the absolute worst and hardest scenarios. In a divorce, fight for your kids; every day you win matters. The judge, the lawyers, your spouse, social workers notice everything. A doctor working days on end during a crisis like our pandemic can make an error, and a nurse can catch him or let it slip. The patient who is dazed and weak fails to become their own advocate and doesn't check to see what they are taking or even fails to speak up when they see what they think is a mistake.

The harder the time, the more forgivable mistakes become, in theory, but in reality the only thing that matters is the result—you win custody, the patient survives. Second place in a divorce means you lose your children; second place in a medical crisis means someone is losing their life.

There are always competitions. Don't be fooled into thinking the competition is not real or the game will be softened for you when things are hardest. The game does not end, the stakes only get graver.

If you want to survive hell, never half-ass anything, never give in to the temptation to relax your standards—especially when you are near the end. It's not over until it's over. Half-assing at the end of a crucible makes you vulnerable. Yes, it will be tough when you can't walk, can't talk, can't think. What happens—win, lose, or horrific accident—is the result of the effort you put in during the most miserable time. That is the key. Effort equals result and environment, and who you are or what you have done before the crucial moment does not matter. Olympic-class swimmers and runners fail Hell Week regularly. Why? They gave less than 100 percent 100 percent of the time. Kids who never played a sport in high school go all out and get through. It's not about how good you are, but how far you will push yourself every second of Hell Week. In life, don't do things halfheartedly. Completely commit yourself at all times. This is the only way to live life.

> Never take a single moment for granted. Not the good times, not even the bad times. Know this: your worst moment during Hell Week is a blessing. It means you are in the game; it means you are walking, living, fighting. If you are in a wheelchair, you are blessed, if your eyes are still open, you can still fight.
>
> —LZ, former Navy SEAL

If you want to survive hell, NEVER half-ass anything!

CHAPTER 12

DAY SIX: PART ONE

If you want to survive hell, prepare to see ghosts.

You hear the paddles dipping in and out of water, you see the edge of your boat and black water. You are hunched over, paddling mindlessly. Your brain is deprived of sleep, calories, and serotonin. It is not functioning properly.

"Dad? No, I'm fine," you hear someone say.

You look to see the man behind you muttering to himself. He continues to row the boat while he stares into space, speaking to someone who isn't there.

"Your dad's not here, mate," one of the other men says, gently shaking him on the shoulder.

The muttering man's eyes fill with life as he comes back to his senses. He glances over at the man who brings him back to reality and then continues rowing, not saying a word.

The predawn hours of Friday morning are unusually cold, and the sky is dark as a set of low-lying clouds blows in off the ocean, obscuring the moon and stars. The surface of the black water shimmers as the lights of downtown San Diego reflect and dance along the surface of the calm water, and the twinkling lights of Tijuana cast an eerie glow on the southern horizon as the team rows south.

At sunset the night before, the remaining teams began a rite of passage called "Around the World," a training event consisting of rowing fifteen miles, starting in the Pacific Ocean, paddling around the island of Coronado, and ending in the southern part of San Diego Bay. Every few miles, the instructors wait on the shore where they order you in and proceed to surf torture and dish out hundreds of push-ups to all the boat crews who commit the unforgivable sin of not arriving first.

After a long, cold, miserable night, you are finally on your last leg of "Around the World," a five-mile journey directly south, where the instructors and a world of hurt will be waiting. You reach new levels of exhaustion as you shiver and row like mindless zombies through the cold black water in your inflatable boat.

You are positioned on the starboard bow position (front right) as you row into the foggy darkness. Your view of the water in front of you is completely unobstructed and you, along with the man across from you, are responsible for guiding your crew in the right direction. You guide your team forward, entering a fog bank, and when you emerge you see a massive marble structure rising up out of the ocean before you. Surprised, but too exhausted to jump or make a scene, you slowly turn your head and look at the other men in your crew, not sure if you have somehow fallen asleep and drifted far off course. Finding them all conscious despite being in different mental states, you quickly realize you are just hallucinating. There is no giant marble structure rising out of the water off Coronado. You know that as soon as you look back again, the marble building won't be there, but you are wrong.

As you turn your head to check, the marble building stands just as real as ever. The ripples from your rowing lap against its walls, creating small white foam splashes. You raise your focus to just above the waterline, and there in perfect detail is the reflection of yourself and your entire boat crew. Knowing what you saw could not be real, you raise your hand to prove to yourself that the reflection isn't real. However, the reflection mirrors your exact movements.

I'm losing my mind, you think, blinking, willing the marble building to go away. But it won't. *What the fuck is this thing?*

You look up, and on the face of the giant structure, about halfway up, you see words chiseled into the monolith. You squint to read the words—first you see your name and then below it your birthdate and the last date you remember, the day you started Hell Week. A sentence is written below the dates: *He was a good son and wanted to be a great soldier.*

You feel a chill. Can this be?

Are you looking at your grave?

The structure you see is, in fact, a giant tomb—like the kind in New Orleans, except it is many stories tall. This thing you're seeing—this tomb—you believe is a tomb to your former life, the person you were before Hell Week began. Or does it mean you are dead and only imagining trying to become a SEAL? What are you becoming? You feel wetness on your face. Is it raining? Or are you crying?

"Hey brother," a voice calls behind you, "just keep rowing, brother. There is nothing there."

You make peace with the odd structure and shoot a few glances at it as you continue to row into oblivion. A few minutes later, you reach the edge of the massive tomb and row past it. You look behind you and watch as the marble walls disappear into the fog and darkness behind your raft.

Your crew continues to row south when from out of the water emerges another structure. This time it is a wooden box sticking about three feet out of the water, with blinking yellow warning lights inside it.

Is this *thing real?* you think. You look over at the man next to you to confirm you aren't going crazy again.

"Hey man, do you see that thing?" you ask him. Navigation buoys and floating piers aren't exactly uncommon in the bay. This looks like some crazy floating warning box.

He looks at you and smiles, assuming you are hallucinating. "What thing?" he asks.

"I see a fucking wall right there," you say. "Or am I just going crazy?"

Seeing the seriousness in your face, he peers out into the darkness, squinting. "No, man. There's nothing out there."

You continue to row right at the wooden structure, which is still plain as day to you. It is a coffin, just floating in the water in San Diego Bay. The lid is open and you can see your father in it, his face and body exactly like when you saw him at the funeral home so many years ago, except now he's covered in crabs that are eating his skull, and his chest is tied from inside the coffin to a buoy. Deciding to trust your buddy, you push on, figuring the worst that can happen is your boat bumps off the structure and then goes around it, or maybe the boat will get punctured by some underwater metal obstacle and you'll have to swim to shore. At that point, you just don't care.

As the parallel wooden beams come closer and closer, you lift your paddle from the water and brace for impact. You count down the distance in your head. *Ten feet.* The yellow blinking lights flash brightly in your face. *Three feet.* You can reach out and touch it now. *One foot!*

Nothing happens. The yellow lights suddenly stop, your father and the coffin he's in disappear, and you continue south into the darkness.

You shake your head in amazement, muttering to yourself: "Thank God, today is the last day of this shit."

Lesson:

The mind can do strange things when it has had to operate with nearly no sleep for an extended period of time, and while under extreme stress. Hallucination is one of the common reactions to these conditions. The lost desert traveler seeing the proverbial mirage is a common human hallucination brought on by dehydration, heat, and lack of sleep. So is the adage of "don't let your mind play tricks on you." When you are doing something uncomfortable, your mind wants to convince you to stop, and will do virtually anything to trick you into doing so.

When under extreme duress, you will see crazy shit. SEAL candidates will often hallucinate toward the end of Hell Week. Some men will break down, terrified and hysterical, and some will even quit. At this point, if your class is solid and full of good dudes, your brothers will not let you quit just because you're hallucinating.

Hallucinations are scary and can make you panic and become paranoid, and in the course of training this can be very uncomfortable and fleeting. Yet it teaches a very valuable lesson, which is when you are under extreme duress you can't always trust what your mind and your senses are telling you. In life when we get paranoid and let our minds play tricks on us, we often do not have the support mechanisms in place to help us to carry on. Succumbing to paranoia and hallucinations and mental debilitation can have a disastrous impact in civilian life, because it erodes trust and breeds unfounded suspicions. When we are in the hellacious periods of our lives—for example, when we think our partners, romantic or business, are cheating—we look for signs of this and begin to find evidence that the paranoia is real. In divorces we think our children are playing angles (and they may be), and our friends may be too. Giving in to either of these is bad. Patients receiving medical care doubt their caretakers, even turn on them.

For all our advances in medicine and science, the mind and its inner workings are still a mystery in many ways. We do not always understand the cause of visions or extreme paranoia. We do know, however, that when we are under extreme duress and pushed physically and mentally to our extremes, the mind will break down. We must be prepared for this and, as harsh as it sounds, be ready to ignore the insane shit we see and carry on, one paddle stroke at a time, if we hope to get out of hell.

> Most of us hallucinated during Hell Week. Don't trust what you see. Trust your brothers with you to keep you safe.
>
> —Ephraim Mattos, former Navy SEAL

If you want to survive hell, prepare to see ghosts.

CHAPTER 13

DAY SIX: PART TWO

If you want to survive hell, follow commands, ignore the harassment.

You continue rowing the raft south until you see the ominous headlights where the SEAL instructors wait for you on the shore like butchers waiting for a delivery of fresh beef. If you thought it would get easier over time, you're learning it doesn't.

Several other boat crews have already arrived before you and are being beaten for not being first, while one crew stands by a bonfire drinking water and getting warm as a reward for having arrived first. It pays to be a winner. And it really sucks to be you.

As your crew rows toward shore, the taunting begins.

"Welcome, gentlemen!" a voice booms over the megaphone in a mock-friendly voice. Naturally this is Joker welcoming you. "So glad you could *finally* join us!" The voice suddenly turns sinister and cruel. "You fuckers have thirty goddamn seconds to get to shore or we are going to fucking destroy you!"

You row as fast as you can, trying to make the completely unrealistic timeline. Time isn't the issue here; they want you to give everything you have even if they are completely unfair to the group and know you will fail anyway.

The taunting and accusations continue like background noise as you reach shore and store your boat next to the others. "You fucking pussies took all goddamn night to get here, because you knew we'd be waiting for you! You decided you didn't want to put out, so you didn't have to deal with us. Well, fuck you!" the Joker screams.

Without being ordered, you instinctively run as a crew to the group of students lying in the mud attempting to do push-ups. The area is called the Tijuana slews. It is where the effluent of the Tijuana River meets the sand and dirt at the extreme southwest corner of the continental United States. The smell from the mud and river permeates the entire area. This is the VGE viral breeding ground. You think to yourself, *At this stage it doesn't really matter*—as your body has already taken it in, and you are likely immune to any new sickness this area can throw at you.

"Negative!" Joker barks at your crew. "Get wet!" He points to the bay, hand shaking with rage.

Your boots sink into the mud and silt as you walk into the pitch-black water and dunk yourself.

Over the next hour, boat crews continue to trickle in, appearing out of the dark water, the exhausted faces and dead eyes of the sailors illuminated by the dancing flames of the bonfire onshore, while the rest of the group are required to conduct exercises and races in the cold, stinking mud.

The sun rises over the foggy bay as you continue to wallow in the filth and mud like pigs. The rising sun signals the beginning of your last day. Covered from head to toe in reeking black mud, you know you are almost done. But being done and being "almost done" are very different things.

At long last, you are ordered to dunk yourselves in the water of the bay and wipe the caked mud off your faces and uniforms. As you rub the filth off yourself in the equally filthy water, you notice the support personnel preparing military rations. It is almost time for a cold, soggy, barely edible breakfast, but you are excited. Every meal you make it to represents one meal closer to the finish.

You roll up your sleeves, cake your hands and mouths with hand sanitizer, and then sit in the cold sand next to your boats and eat the cold, soggy rations. You know this will be your last meal during Hell Week, but you have no idea how miserable the instructors are about to make it. You think you already know the limits of what the SEAL instructors will do to you, but you are about to learn just how very, very wrong you are.

Several students who have become severely ill with VGE request to use the outhouses nearby to relieve themselves. VGE always induces uncontrollable diarrhea, so attempting to hold it in like you would with urine, where if you pee on your-self it's not a big deal, was not an option. You know what will happen and you can't imagine anything worse, so you step up and ask Joker for mercy. "Sir, can the members of our team who are sick with VGE please use the outhouses?" you ask. "I am sorry for the crude language, but I know what will hap-pen. They will shit themselves. They can't help it."

"No," is Joker's reply.

You are not sure if you heard the Joker correctly. "Sir, can you please repeat?" *Those guys will literally shit their pants if they can't use the outhouses, you fucking bastard.* You look at the man sitting next to you a few feet away. His eyes are wide as well. He is one of the sick ones.

The instructor continues, "You can relieve yourself in the water right over there." You look over to see the instructor pointing to the bay.

No longer able to contain their bowels, the sick men wad-dle over to the water's edge, wade in thigh deep, and drop their pants. The rest of you watch in horror as the men proceed to unleash an unholy spray of diarrhea into the water. Unable to eat the brown, soggy mass of processed meat in your hands, you simply look down and stop watching until they finish.

"Feet!" Joker screams as the sick men wade out of the shit-filled water.

The entire class struggles to their feet and stands at attention.

"Everyone into the water." You think you may be hallucinating again as you hear this.

The entire class hesitates and looks at each other in disbelief.

Immediately reacting to our collective disobedience, the instructors spring into action and unleash a torrent of threats and deadly promises and obscenities. The gist of the message is something like, "GET IN THE FUCKING WATER, YOU GODDAMN MOTHERFUCKING PIECES OF SHIT, OR WE WILL FUCKING DROP YOU ALL FROM TRAINING!"

Knowing they are dead serious, you shuffle toward the water. You are in total mental denial of what is happening. You think for sure they will call you back and you will all realize it is just a bluff. How wrong you are.

As a class, you wade out into the stagnant water, which stinks from the diarrhea and urine that has just been deposited into it less than a minute before. You keep your hands out of the water to avoid contaminating them.

The instructors line up on the shore with their arms folded and stare at you through their black sunglasses.

Joker speaks calmly and clearly while the others glare at you in silence. "When we give you an order, you follow it without hesitation or we will drop you from training and you can go be a fucking loser in the regular Navy with all the other fucking losers." He pauses for a moment. "Because of your disobedience, we're going to punish you by playing a little game called 'Hide the Trainee.'"

Your legs feel weak. You want to vomit. You'd cry if it made any fucking difference. This is going too far.

"Hide the Trainee" is a "game" where the entire class has to entirely submerge themselves in the water and remain under it for five seconds. If any part of any one student isn't under the water for the entire five seconds, you lose and have to do it again.

"Down," Joker orders.

Without hesitation, you dunk your entire body into the shit- and filth-infested water, trying not to gag. You count to five and pop to the surface. The filth runs down your face and you try to keep the water from entering your mouth and nose.

"FAIL!" Joker laughs. "One of your classmates fucked you all and didn't go all the way under."

You know there is no real way to tell who it is, or if Joker is even telling the truth. It does not matter.

"Down!"

You dunk yourselves into the filth and repeat the process again and again and again, until the instructors get bored and let you get out of the water.

"Please, continue enjoying your meal, gentlemen," Joker says, affecting a courteous, waiter-like tone. "Let us know if there is anything we can get for you."

The corpsman on duty stands by ready with a massive bottle of hand sanitizer. With a look of shock and bewilderment, he walks around to each of the men in the class and gives everybody big squirts. "Wash off your hands and faces."

Lesson:

Commands are often mixed with insults and mixed messages. In Hell Week, SEAL trainers who will become brothers in arms are constantly fucking with trainees, yelling insults alongside their orders. This is intentional—to make things as stressful as possible while presenting challenges that require focus. They want you to ignore and execute. This is no different than real life. A boss might be a fucking raging asshole who treats you like shit and insults you, but he also might be giving you the correct instructions that you need to execute. The key here is that some things need to get done. The volume with which you are yelled at, the abuse that is sometimes doled out—completely unfair—do not matter. Sometimes nothing at all matters but the command. Get over the insults, the humiliation, ignore them, BUT listen to what matters and do it well, even if it means lying in shit and puke and holding your breath for five seconds.

As a Navy SEAL commander and during my years running the training of SEALs and SEAL candidates, there were some instructors I had to pull back, guys who literally can go psycho when training people who they know one day may fight with them or with their brothers. You of course don't want anyone to die, but it can be good for trainers to take students to the razor's edge. In life, our inclination is to nurture. Even SEALs are this way at heart. We want to build people up. But this can be a disservice. The world is unrelenting and dangerous. You don't want a good guy leading your class during Hell Week. You want a rabid hellhound who will growl and bite and chase you every second of every day and nearly kill you, so you get stronger. You can't take this personally. You have to rise above and trust that guys like me won't let a rogue instructor kill you.

—Ryan Zinke, former Navy SEAL commander

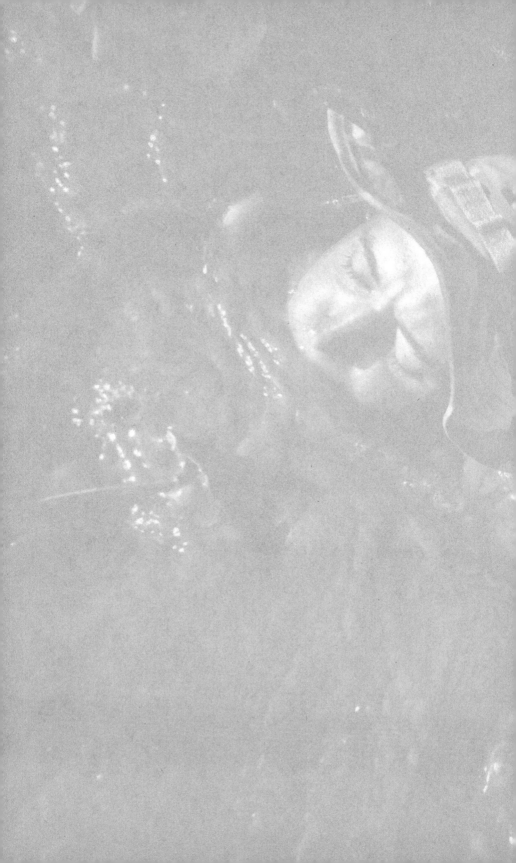

CHAPTER 14

DAY SIX: PART THREE

If you want to survive hell, prepare to go to war before it ends.

Before you know it, you are off again carrying the damn boats on your heads. But this time running north, which means you are headed back toward base. You reach the so-called Demo Pits—a series of pits dug deep into the sand and filled with ocean water—and are ordered to set your boats down and start crawling toward the sound of an instructor blowing a whistle.

Suddenly, the world around you explodes with the sound of several machine guns. Your ears ring and your chest pounds as you drag your body along the ground, only able to see the bottom of the boots of the man in front of you. Your eyes water and you choke uncontrollably, as smoke grenades detonate and fill the air around you with their acrid, chemical stench. One by one, the group crawls into two concrete pipes as the cacophony of explosions and machine guns splits the world around you.

You crawl into the darkness of the pipe behind the man in front of you and immediately force yourself to take a deep breath to avoid the panicked feeling of claustrophobia that begins to build in your chest. The earsplitting noise of the machine guns becomes a rapid thumping noise as you crawl deeper into the pipe.

"Hey man, there's water in here," the man in front of you yells. "You're gonna have to hold your breath."

"Copy that, thanks," you reply.

The man in front of you in the pipe slithers into the water and disappears.

"There's water down here," you shout to the man behind you. "You'll have to go under."

"Roger," the man behind you says.

Waiting only long enough to ensure the man in front of you has enough time to exit the other side of the pipe, you take a deep breath and crawl headfirst into the cold water. A few moments later, you pop up in the center of the Demo Pits, choking on the smoke as machine-gun fire and explosions continue to fill the air. You huddle in the water next to the other men in your class as you watch the rest of your classmates pop up from the pipe and join you.

As you sit in the frigid water, you realize this entire exercise is just a simulation of a combat swimmer operation. After days of running and rowing and crawling through the mud with injuries and no sleep, as SEALs you would still have to conduct an attack on an enemy installation and infiltrate their defenses. Exhaustion, sickness, and injury are no excuse to not complete your mission.

The gunfire eventually stops, and the smoke dissipates as the instructors order you to crawl through the cold water. You crawl back onto the sandy beach, your chafing and misery and exhaustion threatening to break you.

Lesson:

It is no mistake that the last major training cycle during Hell Week involves simulating war. The work of a SEAL is not just to get through grueling shit, it is to get through the worst challenges, to fight through constant struggle across one hell to get to emerge on the other end to a new and more violent hell—the hell of an actual war. Ironically, if you have made it this far, you may be exhilarated by the shock and awe of the real fight. Some will hear the guns booming and rally, feeling a surge of energy. The booming gun may breathe fresh life into your soul. It also may freak you out. Whatever the case, you must be prepared for a war that may be worse and with higher stakes and challenges than you experience when you are in hell.

In civilian life, the kind of hell we sometimes face can be more debilitating than an actual war—husbands and wives who experience the unthinkable loss of a child can find themselves in the middle of the war of divorce when the strain of the loss reveals that the relationship is not as strong as it needed to be.

Just as often, after surviving a medical emergency we are confronted with the war of medical debt, a complete realignment of values and a road to full recovery that is difficult and involves rebuilding one's body. At the end of *The Iliad*, there begins *The Odyssey*.

One hell often leads to another. One war often leads to a new war. Be ready, and if possible, after surviving one hell, let the boom of gunfire inspire you and embrace the new fight with ferocious tenacity.

> The fight only ends when you die. As long as you are physically able to continue to move, you can defeat the enemy. If you hear guns going off, you're alive and be grateful.
>
> —Ephraim Mattos, former Navy SEAL

If you want to survive hell, prepare to go to war before it ends.

CHAPTER 15

DAY SIX: PART FOUR

When you survive hell, be proud and remember those who believed in you.

Line it up going north!" an instructor yells. The group struggles to their feet and moves as quickly as possible to the boats. You wave over your delirious boat crew members who are lost and confused, and then pick up your boat and put it on your heads.

The instructors harass and push you as you run along the beach back toward Coronado Island. Despite your injuries and exhaustion, the instructors refuse to let you slow down or show any sign of slacking. Their standards are high, and they aren't going to let you through easily. You know Hell Week is almost over, but the SEALs demand that you suffer until the very last minute to earn your spot in the training pipeline. Tradition has forged this ruthless rite of passage, and war has confirmed its necessity.

Hell Week ends as suddenly as it begins. You reach the BUD/S training base and have just finished another surf passage race. You stand at attention next to your boats, facing the ocean and ready for the next race, when you are suddenly ordered to "about face."

You turn around to see the entire SEAL instructor staff standing at the top of the sandy berm. The lead instructor that morning is your class proctor. He stands in the middle of the group holding a long flagpole with Old Glory waving in the ocean breeze.

"HELL WEEK IS SECURED!" he yells.

Only the men who have made it through Hell Week can fully comprehend the meaning of these magic words.

"Hooyah!" A scream of triumph erupts from your class.

A deep sense of relief and pride sweeps over you. You turn to the men of your boat crew and shake hands in congratulations. Some cry. Others cheer and hug the man next to them. You just stand in shock with a big, cheesy grin on your face.

The class lines up in three rows. The SEAL instructors file through the lines and shake every one of your hands.

"Congratulations," they each say with a smile and a nod of affirmation. Their torturous, diabolical personas melt away, to reveal that they are just common men who do uncommon things.

As you stand, nearly hobbled, in the line, a man steps in front of you. He is the man who has tormented you more than any other SEAL. "Congratulations," Joker tells you, looking into your eyes and hanging on to your hand. "I would be proud to serve with you in combat. You're a tough mother-fucker." He winks. "Good job."

You are shocked and feel a rush of emotions, but before they can come on and perhaps bring a tear to your eyes, Joker steps away and moves to the next man.

"Okay, gents," your class proctor says. "Congratulations. Once you leave the beach, head over to the medical facility, have the docs check you out, and then go get yourselves a hot shower and some sleep. You've earned it!"

Breaking from your rigid form of attention, you attempt to take a step forward off the beach, but your feet won't work. Your legs suddenly feel as if they have become bags filled with sand. You look around at the other men. They too are experiencing the same phenomenon. Two students suddenly fall over unconscious.

"Corpsmen!" Joker screams.

Corpsmen sprint over to the two unconscious men, and after a quick inspection, they are loaded onto stretchers and their limp bodies are carried from the beach.

"Don't worry, they'll be fine," Joker says to the class, all menace and terror gone from his voice. "Everyone head to medical. This happens all the time."

You will your body forward alongside the other men from your class and eventually make it to medical. You can't understand how walking can be so excruciating and difficult when just minutes before you had been running in the sand while carrying a boat on your head.

You strip down to your boxers and stand in line for your final medical check. Around you, a scene similar to an emergency room after a major disaster unfolds. People are bleeding from multiple areas of their bodies, looking as if they had been dragged behind moving vehicles. Your teammates are covered in cuts and bruises, with some wounds looking very severe. One man's testicles suddenly swell to the size of grapefruits and he is rushed to the front of the line.

You look down at your own tattered, bloody body. You immediately check your sack. You are glad your balls are relatively the same size as when you started, even if they do feel a bit bigger. But your eyes, ankles, and hands begin to swell as you stand in line.

Blood runs down your thighs from the raw chafing areas between your legs, which look more like raw hamburger meat than human skin. The chafing beneath your armpits and around your waist and neck are the same bloody mess. You struggle to keep your eyes open as they pound and pulsate and swell.

A quick check from the corpsman reveals you are "good to go." Your situation is "normal" and, although excruciatingly painful, it won't kill you.

You waddle out of the medical bay in your boxers to see a small group of pre–Hell Week students waiting to help you. You know they haven't been through Hell Week because they each wear the uniform white shirt of a new trainee under their camouflage blouse. They are referred to as "White Shirts."

You also know they haven't gone through it yet, because they have that look in their eyes of shock, fear, and amazement. They have yet to be put through the crucible, the grinder, but they know it is coming, and it is bad.

"Hey man. Congratulations. I'll help you to your room," one of the White Shirts says to you.

You nod in gratitude. "Thanks." Barely audible, your voice sounds hoarse, as if you've been screaming for a week straight.

You follow the eager White Shirt to the courtyard of your barracks and look in amazement at what you see.

Lined up in rows on the ground are several dozen pizzas. You recognize the name of a local pizza joint and think back to the Uber driver who mentioned getting a free pizza if you make it through Hell Week. That pizza might have been donated, but there are no motherfucking more expensive pizzas on earth than the ones lined up waiting for you and your fellow classmates. On top of each pizza box lies a green helmet with the name and class number of each man who has made it through Hell Week. Also lying on top of each pizza box is a neatly folded brown shirt, worn only in BUD/S by those who have completed Hell Week.

"What's your last name?" the White Shirt asks you as he starts looking through the names on the helmets.

You tell him, and after a few moments he picks up a green helmet with your name stenciled on the front and back. Your heart swells with pride as you see your family name on your uniform, knowing that you have been tested as mercilessly as any human in the history of military training and have passed. You are prepared to serve your country well, and have not shamed your family by quitting.

As you are hardly able to keep on your feet, the White Shirt carries your things up the flights of stairs that lead to your barracks room. He holds the door open for you while you walk in.

In the center of the room lies a single mattress with one of your dresser drawers stuck underneath to elevate your feet.

"Oh, wow. You're the only one from your room who made it," the White Shirt says.

You nod and look at the three empty beds where your friends and roommates had once slept. They have all quit.

"Thanks, man. I appreciate it," you say, slightly shocked at how coarse and gruff your voice sounds. It is the voice of a different man.

"Of course. If you need anything or have an emergency, we'll have White Shirts standing outside in the hallway all night." He puts your things down and leaves to go help the next man.

After taking a warm shower and eating a couple pieces of pizza, you find your phone in your personal drawer and lie on the mattress. Electric shocks of pain shoot up and down your spine as you lower yourself to the floor. Later you will learn that you have a ruptured disk in your spine, an injury that will take months to heal and will roll you back to the next class. But you didn't quit, and would not have to relive hell.

You made it this far on the journey to become a SEAL. God-damn it felt good to know that.

You put your feet up onto a drawer that has been left open. You need to keep your feet elevated when you first sleep, so the blood does not drain into your lower extremities and cause edema. It's awkward at first, but you're so damn tired you could sleep with your legs propped up and hanging out of an elephant's ass.

You know you're going to fall asleep soon, so if you're going to call anyone it'd better be quick. You pull the phone onto your chest and tap on the screen, bringing it to life. You think about who to call. You're ashamed to admit that the first name to pop in your head is the girl who you were pretty sure is fucking a buddy of yours back home. Nope. She will not get a text from you—as much as you'd like to hear the voice of a hottie on the other end. In fact—Boom—you delete her contact. Next you think about calling your mom, but you know she'll just ask about how you are doing physi-cally, and you don't want to lie to her, not now, you don't have the strength. You think about texting your uncle who once was in the Coast Guard, the one who seemed like a hero grow-ing up and also the one who pretty much tried to talk you out of challenging yourself with the SEALs. You'll probably see him soon enough, maybe have a glass of eggnog with him next to the Christmas tree. You think about some buddies, but they wouldn't understand or really care about what you've been through. Your mind finally settles on the perfect person, the exact one to whom you should be reaching out. You find the recruiter who talked to you about this journey nearly two years ago and you hit dial. It rings a few times. You have no idea if the man is still in the Navy, if he's a recruiter, or even if he remembers you.

He answers, even though you can hear voices in the background. Sounds like he's at a barbecue. "Hey sailor," he says. "How are you? Everything okay?"

"Yes sir," you say, fresh tears flooding your salted eyes. "Just wanted to let you know Hell Week is secured. Thank you for believing in me, sir."

Lesson:

Making it through Hell Week is an incredible feat, even before the pain subsides, and you are left with a feeling like no other. Pushing yourself—making life intentionally harder—is counterintuitively the way to experience the deepest and most profound joy and accomplishment. You need to recognize this. Even if you are in a zombie state you will feel it. Embrace it—you will and can grow from it, and you should be proud.

Let yourself be proud of what you accomplished and remember those who helped you through—even the bastards who tortured you along the way, like the Joker, whose torment made you stronger. No one can get you through hell but you, and you need to recognize that and acknowledge your incredible accomplishment—and yet you did not do it alone. Your parents who raised you to dare to dream, your friends who helped you along the way, your classmates, your instructors, your God, even the guys who quit helped you keep going in some ways. During your most difficult struggles, it's important to be grateful and to acknowledge the help you received along the way. The more generous you are in your gratitude, the richer you will be when you walk, limp, ride, or are carried out of hell, a free man.

Hell Week captures the very core of what drives a SEAL to beat the odds and win. Reading this book is as close to being as wet and sandy as it gets. For those of you with an interest in becoming a SEAL, do yourself a favor—if you have any doubt, read this book. If you are ready for the ultimate test and to pursue a life of adventure and service that will far exceed any dream you could possibly imagine, then you are ready for hell. Go speak to a Navy recruiter. Your new life awaits you.

—Ryan Zinke, former Navy SEAL commander

THERE IS ALWAYS THE BELL

After securing Hell Week the minds and bodies of Navy SEAL candidates are decimated. The candidate's skin has been literally sanded off his body for six days straight. Most SEALs are covered in sores and dermal abrasions, requiring medical attention. Soft tissue damage is extensive. Muscles and tendons are depleted of nutrients, strained, and the very fibers that bind the human body together are weakened to the point where many SEALs report that it takes a full year for them to feel 100 percent recovered. Bone fractures, spurs, and spinal injuries are common and often only discovered in the wake of Hell Week. Sleep commonly is affected for weeks and months. After Hell Week, SEALs are plagued with nightmares and cold sweats, their minds slipping back into the torture they experienced so intensely for six unrelenting days. And yet with all this long-term impact, after approximately a week of rest, SEAL candidates report back for duty. After completing what is almost certainly the most grueling six-day period of a warrior's life, within weeks SEAL candidates find themselves placed back into another insanely challenging training cycle. It is during phase two when the candidates must complete pool competency, an open circuit of eight extremely difficult dives in which a candidate must master his gear, diving with a blackout mask, diving while under duress, and five other tests designed to assess the candidate's ability to operate calmly when stressed underwater. Like Hell

Week, this training cycle is designed to break students—to weed out the lesser candidates. Fifteen to twenty percent of students in phase two fail at least one of these tests and are rolled back. Should they fail again, they are out of the program and will never wear a trident. Ten percent of these candidates will not pass phase two and move on to phase three of BUD/S: explosives and weapons training. Throughout the entire eighteen months of BUD/S training, the bell remains on hand to be rung by any candidate for any reason.

The vast majority of SEALs who make it past phase two would never dream of quitting, and yet some do ring out. These are candidates who have proven that they possess the ability to endure the hardest times but who come to the realization that the life of a SEAL is one of perpetual risk, pain, and new and increasingly difficult challenges. There is a saying among the SEALs—there is no easy day except yesterday. Most men who want to be SEALs and have completed Hell Week not only understand this mantra but also live by it. Those who do not, ring the bell.

After completing BUD/S, a young man is given a medal, a trident pin, that is hammered into his chest by the hand of a fellow SEAL. As the trident pierces the skin, the young man moves into a class of men who qualify as among the greatest warriors in the history of our planet. And yet to the members of the team to which he has been deployed, that SEAL is an untested new guy. To the veteran warfighters, this man is certainly worthy of respect and the name SEAL, but to these experienced fighters the young man is utterly unproven in combat.

To prepare this freshly minted SEAL for combat the young man will undergo an additional eighteen-month training period known as a work-up. During this time, the SEAL will train with a tightly knit team and then await deployment, at which time the government will send the team to wherever the SEAL and his comrades are needed. Since September 11, 2001, this has often meant being placed in harm's way. For many SEALs, their first deployment will be in a war zone, where on the first real day on the job, religious fanatics, insurgents, and enemy soldiers who have spent twenty years there will be trying to kill him as soon as he arrives. *Welcome back to hell.*

In this environment, this new all-too-real hell, there is no physical bell, no way the SEAL can safely quit and leave when shit gets hairy. Quitting is simply not a viable option. And yet the opportunity to quit on yourself, your teammates, your country, and the citizens of the war zone whose lives you are there to protect looms large. Every second of every day outside of the wire, every step, every breath you take presents an opportunity to quit or fail and to operate at less than 100 percent. To do this, to give up in any way, especially to fail to be in tune with a SEAL's sixth sense for threat, comes with dire consequences—death to you, death to your team, death to innocents, dishonor, and the destruction of our nation's military and political aims. In this moment, from the first perilous day on the job and every moment after that, the suffering of Hell Week pays off. The SEAL now in combat knows that no matter what he and his teammates experience, he has been through worse and together they can and will not only survive, but thrive. Furthermore, and more importantly, the Navy SEAL is sure of one certainty. He will never be defeated if he never quits. And every man with him understands the same.

The threats posed to our health, safety, and security never end. Not for us as humans on this earth, as citizens of the United States, or even as SEALs. There is no time for a SEAL to rest on laurels or relax their vigilance, not after Hell Week is secured, not after BUD/S is complete, not during or after work-ups, or even after the battle is over and the warrior has come home to a grateful nation. I was reminded of this fact on a recent trip to the Navy SEAL training facility in Coronado. Hell Week had been secured the morning of my visit. A few zombies walked the base. Most of the SEALs who had just completed this horrific training lay asleep in bed, feet elevated so as to not let blood pool in their lower extremities. Not three hundred yards from where these men slept, feet in the air, a cool breeze blowing in from the Pacific, was the complex for SEAL Team Three. In the entryway to this facility resides a memorial to my friend Chris Kyle. His kit—his boots, helmet, vest, gun, and gear—is stacked neatly next to other memorials of his fallen comrades.

As we know, Chris spent ten years in the SEAL Teams,

having experienced four deployments in which his life was in near-constant mortal danger. It was only after this that his life was taken while he was performing a charitable act, trying to help a marine recover from post-traumatic stress disorder. It is worth noting that when Chris was shot multiple times by the man he was trying to help, he pursued his attacker. His left hand had been raised in a defensive posture. His right hand was attempting to draw a weapon to fire. Chris was killed, but he never quit, he never stopped fighting, even as his life was taken from him.

As this book nears its conclusion, I will propose a question that I have asked myself every day for over a decade: What can be learned from the SEALs and implemented by people like me who have never experienced, nor ever will experience, what it takes to become a SEAL? In the case of this book, what can we learn and implement from Hell Week? SEALs are undoubtedly exemplary individuals, who by virtue of their training have accomplished something that transcends what most of us will ever experience in normal life.

To understand how to derive lessons from these men and their experiences, I have looked at other examples of how we learn from other extraordinary humans. The Bible—the Old and New Testaments—is replete with extraordinary individuals. From Moses to Mary to King David to Jesus, we are shown examples of leadership, faith, suffering, love, transcendency, rebirth, and wisdom of the ages. Those lessons were first codified by the writers of the Old and New Testaments and then pored over for thousands of years, those actions and lessons reviewed and reflected upon by countless souls yearning to learn how to improve themselves (mortally and immortally) by gaining a deeper understanding of these people, their experiences, teachings, and interpretations of the same. The source of these remarkable learnings is, of course, not limited to Judeo-Christian origins, but also applies to Islam and the life of Muhammad, Buddhism and the Buddha, and all of the world's religions.

In addition to theological examples of how we have studied, codified, and derived lessons from extraordinary people and times, we also have examples of political and military peoples and lessons to look to. The list is long and includes many examples, such as the ancient Greek philosopher kings, the iron mindset of the three hundred Spartans who held off the Persians at Thermopylae, the military and political leaders who saw our planet through two world wars, and countless other extraordinary groups that have shaped the world we live in today. By studying the lives they led, the lessons they taught directly and indirectly, we can become better, deeper, richer, and yet we never need to flight a spear, to bear a cross upon which we will be crucified, or to order the bombing of Hiroshima or Nagasaki. We must be able to learn and benefit without firsthand experience—and in fact, it is our responsibility and necessity.

Since meeting Chris Kyle in a Southern California bar, I have devoted the better portion of a decade of my life to studying and documenting the lives, minds, men, and actions of Navy SEALs. I don't think it is a mistake or an exaggeration to class these men and the lessons that make them who they are among the greatest examples we have to look at over the breadth of humankind. While it is certainly impossible to fully experience what it means to be a Navy SEAL without completing their legendary training, in writing this book I have tried to do my best to define the most important lessons that can be gained during Hell Week. Their crucible.

Summarized in the next section are the lessons of Hell Week explored in detail in this book. Keep them at hand as you experience difficulty in your life. These lessons are applicable to all situations and can help see you through the most difficult times in your life. And if these ten lessons seem overly complex or make your head hurt from trying to read and process them, there are two words that form the foundation of every SEAL. By simply remembering those two words you will be able to endure difficulty beyond your farthest conception, and if you recall them when pursuing your dreams, you will accomplish things you never thought possible. These two words can ensure in life that you will never, ever be beaten by anything. They are the most powerful weapon a SEAL has. If you take anything away from this book or from the SEALs, simply remember these two words: *Never quit.*

—*Scott McEwen, November 2020*

LESSONS FROM THE U.S. NAVY SEALS

Chapter 1 Lesson

Well-meaning others—mom, dad, family, your girl or guy—will rarely understand why you would want to give up security and accomplishment for a chance to risk everything in order to have a shot at your dreams. They will try to dissuade you from attempting a big challenge because they don't want you to get hurt. From them, it comes from a place of love and concern. Other haters will simply try to bring you down. The "safer road" is always the easier choice. This applies to climbing mountains, running marathons, attempting an Ironman, writing a book, volunteering to work with the infected, taking a medicine or vaccine that could either kill you or cure you. The risk you know you need to take, the sacrifice you want to make—these are the steps that those who love you will always try to keep you from making. Only you can make that decision, and once you decide to take on any worthwhile challenge, you will immediately be met with an overwhelming struggle.

Winston Churchill famously told the British people at the

beginning of World War II as Germany set its sight on the United Kingdom, "I have nothing to offer but blood, toil, tears, and sweat." Churchill also said, "The empires of the future are the empires of the mind." I have always enjoyed that quote, because it was truly descriptive of the British Empire at that time. The "empire" that was physically controlled by the British had dwindled to the point of strategic alliances with countries that were no longer militarily controlled by Great Britain. Yet the language, teachings, law, and common heritage ("the collective mindset") of the British that were left with India, Australia, Canada, the United States, and many other former colonies allowed the tiny island to remain alive during a blitz from a continent then controlled wholly by Nazi Germany. Churchill's words have nothing to do with the Navy SEALs, but in some respects they could not be more appropriate. For those who want to join the SEALs, or take up a great adventure or a needed risk to rise above their circumstances, doing so will put them straight into a form of suffering and hell. You will be unable to control the environment you are forced to place your body into—in fact, you will be forced to endure physical challenges and suffering no sane person would ever "voluntarily" walk into. That is the first step. The next step is to realize that your mental fortitude will lay the foundation for the empire of your future.

Here is the truth. If you want to do anything different it'll freak people out. If you want to be a SEAL, it'll scare the hell out of some people. When I decided to join the SEALs, I was still in high school and had grown up in a devoutly religious Christian sect that practiced pacifism. Initially, my decision to join the SEALs effectively cut me off from my friends, my parents, my family. I now have my family back, but to pursue this life I had to be willing to walk away from many people who I loved and cared about. Not everyone will walk the path with you, let alone stand by while you pursue your dreams. You must pursue them anyway.

—Ephraim Mattos, former Navy SEAL
and humanitarian

If you want to achieve greatness you'll have to go through hell to get it. So ignore everyone, listen to your heart, and embrace the suck.

Chapter 2 Lesson

In life and in the SEALs, we must always prepare as diligently as possible for what we know will happen. A trainee who does not train ahead of time for BUD/S is an arrogant fool begging to lose out on fulfilling a lifelong dream. Likewise, a civilian who does not prepare for goals in his or her life is equally as foolish and arrogant. We do our homework, we study for our tests, and we rehearse our presentations, so that when we are put to the test we perform. And yet it is equally foolish and arrogant to believe we have control over fate, God, weather, or a little germ that crawled up our asses. We must also prepare for the unexpected to happen.

The good thing in preparing for the unexpected in life and in the SEALs is to have a mindset. Know what the ultimate move is that you can fall back on if all of your plans fail. In the case of the SEALs, the rule "never quit" is enough, and having a simple mantra when shit hits the fan can have a grounding effect, quiet the mind, and give you confidence that no matter what, you can complete the course. In life, the mindset needs to match the circumstance. The challenges of enduring a failing marriage are very different from those of launching a new start-up. That said, a simple mantra such as *No matter what I will be okay* or *No matter what I will not quit* will usually work when you find yourself encountering the unexpected.

The vast majority of retired SEALs I know are extremely successful at whatever line of work they choose. Some choose to complete their education and become doctors, physicians' assistants, businessmen, you name it. A thought comes to mind of me going to Montana to attempt to help my friend Ryan Zinke become a U.S. congressman from that great state. Montana is generally known as being fairly conservative (although that has unfortunately changed some as of late due to Californication), and thus the winner of the Republican primary is oftentimes favored to win the sole congressional seat for a state the size of the entire northeastern section of this country. Ryan was running against some other former military members who had significantly more name recognition than he did. But I will tell you what they did not have—the drive of a former officer at SEAL Team Six. To state it simply, you could not outwork this individual, and I witnessed personally how he beat his competition, because that is exactly what he did. He got up earlier, drove longer, took more meetings, did more interviews, slept less, and drove his team supporting him (myself included) to do the same. If he had no time to work out, he would drop and do a hundred push-ups and sit-ups, and he would incentivize you to do the same. Not only did he win the primary, he won the general election. By the end I knew why, as not only is Ryan a great patriot and son of Montana who deserved to represent his beloved state in Congress (and ultimately be appointed to the office of secretary of the interior), but he outworked the competition. He personified the first and last rule of the SEALs: Never quit!

Preparation is everything in a team. You must have your shit together—your kit, your A, B, and C plans, your strength, your tactics—everything matters. It is a sin not to prepare, because if you don't prepare to the absolute best of your ability, you are putting your life and, more importantly, the lives of others in danger. That said, no amount of well-prepped gear, no amount of workouts, no plan or backup plan is anything compared to how you mentally prepare. The good news

is that mental preparation and your ability to calm
yourself and come up with a plan when you are down
can save you from nearly any situation, no matter how
fucked you are, how outgunned you are. Keep clear
between the ears and you'll get through anything.

—Ryan Zinke, former commander at SEAL
Team Six, U.S. congressman, and
secretary of the interior

Chapter 3 Lesson

We have all heard the expression "shock and awe." It is a tactic often employed by militaries where through the use of overwhelming force the enemy is surprised, demoralized, and loses the will to fight. The enemy literally is filled with shock and awe by the display of might and power.

This principle does not apply only to the military. Shock and awe is used in sports. Think of what happens in a football game when a team comes out on fire and quickly takes a 14-point lead: The opponent often gives up and the game is over before it gets going. The principle of shock and awe is used in business, in negotiation, in family and social interactions. Lawyers often try to use shock and awe in their cases—trust me, I have.

The effects of shock can also be seen in how most of us react to natural disasters and acts of God. Just search the internet for "tornado aftermath stories" and you can see it in the faces of men and women looking at their obliterated homes. Disease—especially viral disease—seems to act the same way. Right now, much of the world is in a state of paralysis caused by shock and awe, as if the coronavirus has caught us with a vicious uppercut.

Hell Week too begins with carefully choreographed shock and awe. The intent is to freak those out who are likely to quit, to overwhelm the students and make them believe they cannot possibly survive the rest of Hell Week, if it is like this first day and night. While it is certainly startling and awful, the truth about the tactic of shock and awe is that the effects wear off rather quickly. If you don't quit, the shocking violence of action with the start of Hell Week rings hollow after a while. You get used to it.

In World War II, Britain was nearest to capitulation in the first few days of bombing. The "Blitz," aka blitzkrieg, which is German for "lightning war," was on. For fifty-seven nights London was bombed mercilessly. After the shock and awe wore off and the English people dug in and showed their grit, it was Adolf Hitler who was shocked that the English were not giving in so easily. The football team that keeps its head on straight, even after a huge deficit, can come back. The family that loses their home after the tornado or hurricane can find new shelter—ideally on safer ground. There is a point when lawyers shouting becomes merely hot air, and there is a point when we figure how to live with a pandemic.

To survive this initial onslaught, the best way forward is often to just stay calm and keep crawling, even if it means you must crawl through puddles of your own puke.

When the guns start popping off in battle most people freeze up. It is a natural reaction to such extreme stress. When people get knocked down after being wounded, that's when they go into shock. When the untrained warrior realizes he is shot, and you let the shock take over, that is when he begins to die. When things go bad and overwhelm us—that is when we tend to stop. What Hell Week taught us as SEALs is to keep moving, no matter what. You can always inch forward, you can always make progress even if you are pulling yourself forward with your teeth. Never ever stop. When I was shot in the leg during a battle in Mosul, Iraq, the initial shock to my mind and my body was substantial. Then, after almost being run over by a tank assisting us in the operation, I instinctively went into my SEAL training mode; the round that had gone through my leg had not hit bone or a major artery. I was still able to put some weight on the leg. There was no QRF [Quick Reaction Force] in this battlefield, and the enemy rounds were still pouring in relentlessly. I literally had to get myself, and my team of fellow warriors, off the battlefield, or we were done. My SEAL training took over, and I repeated to myself to get through the pain and the confusion, "I am a fucking Navy SEAL, I am a fucking Navy SEAL." It worked. I reengaged and got back into the fight for both my life and that of those we were trying to save in Mosul from ISIS. The SEAL instructors were not standing over me screaming "RING THE BELL," but they may as well have been, because I realized why they had the bell. When you are in battle, "the bell" (quitting) cannot exist as an option... period.

—Ephraim Mattos, former Navy SEAL,
author of *City of Death*

Chapter 4 Lesson

Mindset is everything. Mindset *is* everything. Your mindset determines how you interpret the world, your senses, your existence. When you feel pain, extreme pain, you can choose to succumb to it, ignore it, or even thrive off it. Your mindset is entirely under your control, in fact it is the *only* thing you can control. This is true in life as it is in the SEALs.

You made it through day one of Hell Week because you had won the mental battle before the first shots of Hell Week were fired. You mentally were ready and your body—fucked up as it was—had no choice but to follow. And Price's did too. You both made it thanks to what was in your head.

We can win or lose before the trial begins. Having the courage to face our fears requires acknowledging weakness and having a plan to rise above it. Most people are defeated before the battle begins, primarily because they do not honestly take stock of their fears and weaknesses. They have no plan and believe that because they have won most of their lives before a true test, they will win again. What they don't realize is that they have spent their lives relying on luck and environment—birth, schools, connections—to carry them through. They expect to win and have committed a grave blunder of ego.

Ignoring the reality of our challenges and pretending they will not be hard or that we can easily surmount a real challenge is dangerous and foolish. Not realistically assessing risk is how you get your ass kicked early in a fight, how you lose a court case, or how the likeliest of candidates almost quits less than twenty-four hours into the six-day challenge.

We often think we can get by with bravado, but in a true test it will always fail if all we have is our oversized ego, misplaced confidence, and energy. We must avoid this mistake by assessing our weaknesses and limitations and figuring out how we will get through to victory. Taking the first step toward this can seem daunting. And most of us do not engage in activities where our plan to make it through a day is "let them drag me out of here." But the lesson is the same. No matter what your challenge is, know where you are weak and plan for victory. When you have a plan to follow, you know what to do when shit goes haywire, you know—literally—where to place your next step. When you know what to do in the worst-case circumstance, you can then take that step and your body follows!

Have the courage to begin, to face failure, to knowingly throw yourself into what amounts to torture. When you knowingly do this, it only follows that you will come out victorious.

As a Navy SEAL officer one of my jobs was that I led phase one of BUD/S for five years. I get asked all the time what determines whether a candidate makes it all the way through BUD/S to become a SEAL—is it their training, their physicality, their smarts, their innate athleticism? After seeing thousands and thousands of men try and the few make it, I can say without question, the greatest factor is that the SEALs that make it simply decide to make it. They make a choice. No matter what, I will make it. And they never back off. This is the SEAL mindset. It can be made at any point in BUD/S. The best make it before they arrive. Some make it midway through. It doesn't matter. All make it. And once the decision is made, it is forged in steel.

—Lieutenant Commander "Iron" Ed Hiner, former Navy SEAL and training officer at BUD/S

If you want to survive hell, first win the battle in your mind and your body will follow.

Chapter 5 Lesson

Being a SEAL requires that you never leave a fellow brother behind, that you carry the weight of others. And yet an important part of the SEAL training, a very harsh part, is letting go of whatever holds you back, which could be a behavior or a person who does not deserve to be part of your team.

There is a difference between quitting and letting go—a very important difference. The SEALs never quit, they never quit on themselves or their team, their brothers, those who are mentally committed to the same goals and objectives. But when someone is poisonous, selfish, who is just a drag and playing upon your sympathy, SEALs cut them loose. Let them do what they want—let them *try* to take the easy way out of hell.

The truth, however, is there is no easy way out of hell. Those whom you let quit because they are pulling you down will get the momentary relief they seek. They will get handed the coffee and blanket. The SEALs who want to stay in hell, who want to fight their way through hell and not cheat their way out, will never let you down. Don't let go of these people. Let go of the others, and the true warriors will thrive.

In life these are the coworkers who talk a good game but never commit, the people who say they want to help you but in the end only hurt you. You know who these people are. They are the ones who play on your sympathies, who suck the most of your energy and never give back. They only give excuses. Let them go.

The men of the team are ultimately responsible for the success or failure of the mission. When one man is unable to carry out that mission during training/qualification, what good will he be in battle? Not only will he compromise his own effectiveness, but he will compromise every man on the team in the event he must be helped and/or extracted (carried) from the field of battle. This is different from the ethos of "leave no man behind." Instead it is the understanding that if he is willing to quit during training, and thereby compromise the team, he will also be willing to quit during operations, where far more is at stake. Even after you are a member of the SEALs and have received your trident, you are still evaluated by your reputation (your "rep"), and every SEAL has one.

I'm reminded of the life, and ultimate death in battle, of SEAL Michael Monsoor. Michael was killed when he jumped on a grenade that had been thrown at him and his teammates in Iraq. Even though he could have easily gotten away from the blast and saved himself, he chose to cover the grenade and thereby attempt to save the lives of the other men on his team. The following is a copy of the citation that led to his posthumously receiving the Medal of Honor, our nation's highest award for gallantry:

For conspicuous gallantry and intrepidity at the risk of his life above and beyond the Call of Duty while

serving as Automatic Weapons Gunner for Naval Special
Warfare Task Group Arabian Peninsula, in support of
Operation IRAQI FREEDOM on 29 September 2006.
As a member of a combined SEAL and Iraqi Army
sniper overwatch element, tasked with providing early
warning and stand-off protection from a rooftop in an
insurgent-held sector of Ar Ramadi, Iraq, Petty Officer
Monsoor distinguished himself by his exceptional
bravery in the face of grave danger. In the early
morning, insurgents prepared to execute a coordinated
attack by reconnoitering the area around the element's
position. Element snipers thwarted the enemy's initial
attempt by eliminating two insurgents. The enemy
continued to assault the element, engaging them with a
rocket-propelled grenade and small arms fire. As enemy
activity increased, Petty Officer Monsoor took position
with his machine gun between two teammates on an
outcropping of the roof. While the SEALs vigilantly
watched for enemy activity, an insurgent threw a hand
grenade from an unseen location, which bounced off
Petty Officer Monsoor's chest and landed in front of
him. Although only he could have escaped the blast,
Petty Officer Monsoor chose instead to protect his
teammates. Instantly and without regard for his own
safety, he threw himself onto the grenade to absorb the
force of the explosion with his body, saving the lives of

his two teammates. By his undaunted courage, fighting spirit, and unwavering devotion to duty in the face of certain death, Petty Officer Monsoor gallantly gave his life for his country, thereby reflecting great credit upon himself and upholding the highest traditions of the United States Naval Service.

We all will limp along. We all need a hand at some point. We all suck at some point. But men like Michael Monsoor don't boat duck. SEALs don't. And those who habitually do so deserve to be cut loose.

If you want to survive hell, learn to let go but never quit.

Chapter 6 Lesson

To be a SEAL and to survive in the hardest times, you must be able to adapt to the situation and accomplish your mission, even when this means doing the difficult thing of running someone out of your crew. It has to be done, but who will step up and take charge? That person is you.

A portion of the Navy SEAL Creed says it best: "We expect to lead and be led. In the absence of orders I will take charge, lead my teammates and accomplish the mission. I lead by example in all situations."

Take charge, don't be afraid to evolve and change who you are, and don't let others' past expectations of you dictate your future. Team-ability, adaptability—you can't do it alone. Others need you too. Break out of your comfort zone and adapt who you are.

Leaders naturally gravitate toward the challenge. Even in failure, they are looked upon as ones who did everything they could to win. This is the quality respected in life. And these people in the teams eventually do win.

In life, like in the teams, during the most difficult times we will see an opportunity to step up and lead, even if we are not naturally leaders. When we see the way forward, we must act, we must change in order to succeed and overcome. This is about stepping up in these insane situations. You *can* lead. You *will* lead if you overcome fear and doubt and speak up. And best of all, you will feel yourself begin to change. You will recognize qualities and strengths in yourself you did not realize you had. They come out when you act. Stop thinking, take the lead.

> During Hell Week, the focus is on survival—students demonstrating they have what it takes to get through this incredibly difficult training cycle. We don't expect much in terms of quality of performance or leadership during this week, but when we see it, it is noted. So, when a kid, especially an enlisted kid still in his teens, shows he can lead during Hell Week, you know you

have the makings of an exceptional SEAL candidate and
human.

—Ed Hiner, Navy SEAL retired lieutenant
commander and BUD/S instructor

Chapter 7 Lesson

Every hurricane has an eye. In the middle of a horrible life-
threatening storm, there is a spot of calm, of bright warm
light. A surreal reprieve in the middle of hell when we are
tempted to think the storm has passed. We relax, let our guard
down, and perhaps even believe the storm really has passed.
But then the black clouds return, the storm closes in around
us and mercilessly demolishes our homes and demoralizes us.

We curse the eye of the storm as a cruel trick, and yet many
of us try to live our lives chasing it, constantly trying to stay in
the calm center of an otherwise terrifying event. We seek out
shortsighted momentary wins, but lose the greater battle. We
work hard at our jobs to be complimented, then relax instead
of working harder. We get a pat on the back, but lose the promotion. Lawyers have a good day in court, feel confident, and
then fail to prepare for the next day and get their asses handed
to them. A salesman in a slump has a good few days, splurges
on drinks with his clients, and then misses his monthly quota.

For SEALs, medical checks exist to save lives by screening
for very serious problems that can develop. They are also a

tool to encourage the uncommitted to drop out while supposedly keeping their dignity. The opposite is true. In fact, most SEALs have more respect for the sailor who quits in front of his class than the one who weasels out of the program with a medical issue that he could have fought through.

And yet the eye of the storm is seductive. When we feel the warmth, we all are tempted to linger, but just remember the eye never lasts. When you walk back out into real life and get sprayed in the face with ice-cold water, you will feel it more painfully. Do not use the momentary reprieve in the battle as an excuse to rest. Make use of the time to batten down the hatches. When you are given a breather and have a chance to quit or give in to temptation, use the time to mentally recommit.

You get killed when you let your guard down. This is true in life and in war. In life, you get killed when you get on the expressway and space out. The most dangerous times during a mission are when there is a lull in the fight, when a dynamic changes, when there is a gap in focus. That is when mistakes are made or the enemy does something unexpected. Continuity of focus is so important. The normal work-up time leading up to a deployment, in other words the time SEALs spend training for deployment, is twelve to eighteen months. Think about that. SEALs will take a year and a half of hard, continuous training to prepare for the time they go to war. During Hell Week, which is unbelievably intense, any pause in training is a chance to lose focus, to make a mistake, to give in to the temptation to quit. Keep your head in the game, always.

—Chris Sajnog, SEAL instructor

If you want to survive hell, beware of momentary comfort and don't ever let your guard down.

Chapter 8 Lesson

In life and in the SEALs, injustice, failed expectations, and empty promises are not just common—they are the rule. Life is *not* fair, ever. We all know Lady Luck is an unfair bitch. Both bad and good luck—physical health, athleticism, looks, wealth, where you stand in the path of a sniper's bullet—are doled out indiscriminately. In reality, often good luck goes to those who don't need it and the rest of us catch the shit and have to fight and scrap to get anywhere close to even. What is worse, when luck is taken out of the equation, when the field is as fair as possible, the rules of the game disproportionately favor the winners. This is really important to understand—life gives more good shit to winners and destroys losers, even the ones who are just a step or two behind the best of the best.

Those in the lead get rewarded and get ahead; those who struggle fall behind, and then they get their asses kicked so they fall further and further behind, until winning is hopeless, and you will never ever get a break until you can get ahead. This is not an aphorism that contains a truth—this is THE TRUTH. No matter how hard you work or deserving you are, the winners get paid. If you don't win, you don't get paid. You eat shit or, in the case of Hell Week, a boot full of sand.

You need to have a thick skin, perseverance, and a never-quit attitude in order to get by. But there comes a point in life and in hell and during Hell Week when simply limping along is a liability. The weak—the injured, the out of shape, the poor bastards with pneumonia and VGE—are the ones who are preyed upon and culled out of the herd. It's not their fault they got sick, but they lost all the same and the world pounced.

This is a very cruel truth about life that is deeply important to understand. When you are sick, suffering, and down and out you can NEVER count on getting a fucking break, and when you do it is pure luck, quite often the luck of where you were born and who you were born to. Most of us are not lucky. This is why you can never stop trying to win.

Life, at least in the United States, operates like the stock market. The stock market does not give a Wall Street trader who is down on his luck a break—ever. The trader eats what he kills, and the more he kills, the more he eats and the more he can kill. Or he goes fucking broke and into debt trying. The unlucky bastard who gets cancer also gets the medical bills, often loses his job or can't work, winds up broke, and if he's really unlucky, maybe he even gets left by his wife for a younger, healthier guy. Life is fucking unfair.

Countries, and the far leftist politicians in the United States, often try to level the playing field with the intention of giving the same, or similar, to all. This premise is at the heart of socialism and communism, and the truth is, once governments "level the playing field" and socialize, the ONLY ones who win are the thugs, bosses, and insiders. Look at Russia, Venezuela, Cuba, or AOC's inner circle.

Capitalistic democracies like the United States are rare. Life here can be ruthless, but it is the fairest system of them all. And you must, in any and all circumstances, fight your way to the front. Once you get to the front, you better fucking stay there, because as hard as it is to get to the front, it is much, much, much harder and much shittier to try to keep up, much less make up ground once you have fallen behind. Again, the race does not end when there is suffering. Marathons do not stop running when participants die of heatstroke or heart attacks, let alone when some poor bastard shits their pants or twists an ankle. In this race, if you slow down you will lose. And when your life hangs in the balance, losing cannot be an option. Let someone else die.

I repeat: Perseverance is the only way to combat and defeat injustice. Life's not fair, but mentally preparing for the unfairness will get you through. The fastest guys got to rest, while the slower ones were beaten more. "The rich get richer." Fight your way to the top. The cards may be stacked against you and life may suck, but don't give up. There is no individual, from billionaire to shoeshine stand operator, who has not failed and received injustice in the process. The billionaire generally just kept swinging.

> The brotherhood among SEALs is unbelievably strong, stronger than any other on earth, I believe. And, counterintuitively, I think the reason for this is that as SEALs we all know we are fundamentally alone in this life. We know this because some of us come home without a scratch, some come home in a bag or busted into pieces. We must support each other. Yet we all will be tested on our own and, most importantly, we will all face our Maker alone. That thought should stay with you every step.
> —Ephraim Mattos, former Navy SEAL

If you want to survive hell, it pays to be a winner.

Chapter 9 Lesson

Difficult times will drain us in mind, body, and spirit, and if we are to survive, we must nourish ourselves. The 15,000 calories a day that a trainee will burn during Hell Week is an extreme and obvious example of how a body is depleted, and it is also an extreme and obvious example of what it needs to keep going—food. If a trainee does not feed himself, he will not be able to complete Hell Week. This is very simple to understand. Every time an aspiring SEAL swallows some calories during this ordeal, he's putting gas in the tank of the car that will get him to the other side of hell.

In life, the same principle applies, but what we need is not as obvious as what we are using up. After all, food is rarely exactly what we need. In my own life, I gained twenty pounds during my second divorce. I certainly didn't need more calories. What I lost and needed was a sense of family and God, and I temporarily replaced those elements with junk food and booze.

It is so vital that we become aware of what we are losing during the difficult periods of our lives. If we can get precise and understand what we need, like the SEALs know the calories they require to make it through a day, we can seek out the right elements to feed ourselves.

What is more, when we are in our own hell, we do not have instructors with us ensuring we take care of our bodies by force-feeding us every six hours. Instead, we have friends, family, and spiritual leaders who guide us, or, in the case of many, we have false friends and leaders who misguide us. Just like with what we put in our bodies and into our souls, we need to make sure the people closest to us, our "instructors" who intentionally or unintentionally inform our lives, are the kinds of people who will give us what we need. As much as trainees in Hell Week may suffer under their trainers, they know and trust them to provide the right food for the task. We too must find those proven people, cut out the bad ones, and then help the good family, friends, and spiritual leaders to understand what we need as we trust that they will help guide us to it.

> It's really simple. You need to be tough to be a SEAL. You need to be smart if you want to stay in the game, and this means taking care of yourself. You're a fucking asshole and a fool if you disrespect your body. Eat, motherfucker.
>
> —DZ, former Navy SEAL

If you want to survive hell, eat.

Chapter 10 Lesson

It is all too easy to become so centered on our own pain and struggles in life that we forget others are going through hard times. But when we take a step back and see how we can help others we find not only purpose, but also lifelong friends.

If you can get a group of people to work together relentlessly and selflessly toward a common goal where a person would rather die than let down a teammate, that group will always be a greater force to be reckoned with. There must be a point of no return where you commit all to accomplish the goal. When you reach that point you are unbeatable.

If you want to survive hell, fight alongside your true brothers, not against them.

You will complete this training not alone, but as a team. Or you will not complete it at all.

There is a phenomenon with the SEALs that I have witnessed time and time again. It really doesn't matter how badly you fuck up, as long as you fuck *somebody else* up. In other words, when a SEAL does something really bad—say, for example, literally kills somebody—that does not automatically cause expulsion from the team. As long as the person killed was not a team guy, or family of a team guy.

Witness, for example, the case of Eddie Gallagher. Eddie was accused of killing an injured ISIS member who was in the custody of coalition forces. Not exactly Geneva Convention compliant—but the SEALs couldn't really have cared less. In fact, one of his teammates (a medic) ended up taking responsibility for the death, after he was given immunity from prosecution by the Navy. Arguably this was somewhat of a predictable event.

While I was not there, and can only speculate on the exact discussion, I can envision the consultation with the lawyer leading up to the testimony of the SEAL who was given immunity.

SEAL: Let me see if I understand this: I can say whatever I want, and take responsibility for anything up to and including having a part in the death of this ISIS member, and cannot be prosecuted for the act?
Lawyer: Yes, that is correct.
SEAL: Okay, I did it. I finished him.

When this graphic and life-changing testimony was released from the trial, I was neither shocked nor even amazed. It was essentially code. One teammate had the opportunity to cover his buddy's back (six), and he did it. Was the testimony given true? I don't know that either, but it really did not matter in SEAL terms. It was effective in eliminating the threat then existing on another teammate whom you were in battle next to. The more interesting dynamic is that even though Big Navy elected to prosecute Gallagher, even though the case was suspect from day one, they failed to understand the dynamic of the SEALs/Hell Week mentality.

Loyalty and brotherhood are values we should cherish and strive toward. Instead, loyalty and brotherhood in modern times, and in the media, have become buzzwords for proving bad behavior, covering up and excusing mistakes. In this world we live in of "me too" takedowns that occur decades after a supposed event, executives can never know who will tear them down, and the perception is that anyone who wants to see loyalty is looking for an excuse. First, expecting loyalty from your teammate—even if that means publicly covering up mistakes—is not altogether a bad thing. The reality is we need to be able to make mistakes and improve. Also, brothers who are loyal to each other do not let them make mistakes. SEALs who see fellow SEALs failing to live up to the standards of the trident step in and work with their brother to bring him up to the mark.

In civilian life, successful teamwork is based on trust. There CANNOT be a successful team without trust. You don't have to like, admire, or even respect your teammates to accomplish a mission, but you have to be able to rely on them to do their part in the mission—that is trust. Loyalty, support, helping to take your teammates up to a higher level is what good brothers (and sisters) do—these are extensions built upon the basis of trust. The way to win trust and win more missions is to become more trustworthy, more loyal, more supportive in the face of disaster, more sacrificing—these are the qualities that will make you a better person, a better leader, a better teammate, and a better brother and will lift you out of the hardest times and propel you toward success in any theater.

Monday morning quarterbacking seems to be a cottage industry in our modern world. "He should have thrown this pass." "She should have made this objection during trial." Blah, blah, blah. Perhaps Teddy Roosevelt said it best:

It is not the critic who counts; not the man who points out how the strong man stumbles, or where the doer of deeds could have done them better. The

credit belongs to the man who is actually in the arena,
whose face is marred by dust and sweat and blood;
who strives valiantly; who errs, who comes short again
and again, because there is no effort without error
and shortcoming; but who does actually strive to do
the deeds; who knows great enthusiasms, the great
devotions; who spends himself in a worthy cause;
who at the best knows in the end the triumph of high
achievement, and who at the worst, if he fails, at least
fails while daring greatly, so that his place shall never
be with those cold and timid souls who neither know
victory nor defeat.

This is why I have made it my life's passion to help men
and women of the military in need—particularly SEALs. Perhaps that is why they trust me. I honor those who have stepped
up and made the sacrifice to get in the arena for our country.
I don't second-guess the reasons for their actions in combat. I
was not there; I did not see or go through the hell they did.
But I am keenly aware that they went through that hell for
you and me to live a better life with our families and children
here. For that reason, I never second-guess decisions made on
a battlefield. As an American I believe I owe this to our brothers and sisters, sons and daughters who made the decision to
serve. We have seen more men and women prosecuted for war
crimes in the last twenty years than in the entirety of U.S. history, all wars. And this is bullshit. It is a reflection of those who

served being second-guessed by those who have never set foot on the field of battle, aka the arena. "Rules of engagement" have been used to prosecute those who would not let a brother die, even if it meant a court-martial for his acts. This does not bode well for our country, or those who would give their lives in defense of its Constitution. That is why I defend them to a fault.

I believe the same respect and support should be given to the men and women who are in law enforcement here in the United States. It has become all too in vogue for people to run down the police for alleged brutality, racial animus, and related criticisms. The majority of the cases that have been alleged to be examples of "bad behavior" by the police in fact are not evidence of anything but the half-cocked press trying to inflame the populace for their own political positions. The reality is that our police are many times placed into positions every bit as dangerous and kinetic as our warfighting community. One must seriously consider what this does for the ability of the military and the police to recruit our finest in the future. Who wants to do the job with the knowledge that there is a very real possibility you could be prosecuted for it?

The bottom line is that the politicians and the press second-guessing every use of force by our military and our police degrades their readiness to do the job they were hired to do, that is, take out the bad guys.

If you want to survive hell, become a better brother.

Chapter 11 Lesson

Despite pain and hardship, SEALs are expected to keep moving and always stay competitive. Defeat is never an option. They are expected to give 100 percent effort 100 percent of the time. The consequences of not going all out in war are obvious. You can get killed, you can get your teammates killed, and you can fail in your mission. But the truth is in life there are many ways to give up and suffer both metaphorical and real deaths. In the SEALs and in life, when a dickhead makes a bad choice—even in a closely monitored training exercise surrounded by medics—the results can be catastrophic. Worse, when we let our guards down and perform at less than 100 percent, others, innocent people, can get injured. A mechanic who rebuilds a motor with hundreds of parts but fails to tighten one bolt can set in motion events that will lead to disaster and maybe death, even dozens of deaths if, say, the lost bolt is in an engine of a 747.

We must be vigilant always—and we must have each other's backs. Even when we experience the worst and hardest times—the most hellacious shit—it becomes paramount not to become apathetic and lose our edge. Retain your edge by fighting to win and give 100 percent, even in the absolute worst and hardest scenarios. In a divorce, fight for your kids; every day you win matters. The judge, the lawyers, your spouse, social workers notice everything. A doctor working days on end during a crisis like our pandemic can make an error, and a nurse can catch him or let it slip. The patient who is dazed and weak fails to become their own advocate and doesn't check to see what they are taking or even fails to speak up when they see what they think is a mistake.

The harder the time, the more forgivable mistakes become, in theory, but in reality the only thing that matters is the result—you win custody, the patient survives. Second place in a divorce means you lose your children; second place in a medical crisis means someone is losing their life.

There are always competitions. Don't be fooled into thinking the competition is not real or the game will be softened for you when things are hardest. The game does not end, the stakes only get graver.

If you want to survive hell, never half-ass anything, never give in to the temptation to relax your standards—especially when you are near the end. It's not over until it's over. Half-assing at the end of a crucible makes you vulnerable. Yes, it will be tough when you can't walk, can't talk, can't think. What happens—win, lose, or horrific accident—is the result of the effort you put in during the most miserable time. That is the key. Effort equals result and environment, and who you are or what you have done before the crucial moment does not matter. Olympic-class swimmers and runners fail Hell Week regularly. Why? They gave less than 100 percent 100 percent of the time. Kids who never played a sport in high school go all out and get through. It's not about how good you are, but how far you will push yourself every second of Hell Week. In life, don't do things halfheartedly. Completely commit yourself at all times. This is the only way to live life.

> Never take a single moment for granted. Not the good times, not even the bad times. Know this: your worst moment during Hell Week is a blessing. It means you are in the game; it means you are walking, living, fighting. If you are in a wheelchair, you are blessed, if your eyes are still open, you can still fight.
>
> —LZ, former Navy SEAL

If you want to survive hell, NEVER half-ass anything!

Chapter 12 Lesson

The mind can do strange things when it has had to operate with nearly no sleep for an extended period of time, and while under extreme stress. Hallucination is one of the common reactions to these conditions. The lost desert traveler seeing the proverbial mirage is a common human hallucination brought on by dehydration, heat, and lack of sleep. So is the adage of "don't let your mind play tricks on you." When you are doing something uncomfortable, your mind wants to convince you to stop, and will do virtually anything to trick you into doing so.

When under extreme duress, you will see crazy shit. SEAL candidates will often hallucinate toward the end of Hell Week. Some men will break down, terrified and hysterical, and some will even quit. At this point, if your class is solid and full of good dudes, your brothers will not let you quit just because you're hallucinating.

Hallucinations are scary and can make you panic and become paranoid, and in the course of training this can be very uncomfortable and fleeting. Yet it teaches a very valuable lesson, which is when you are under extreme duress you can't always trust what your mind and your senses are telling you. In life when we get paranoid and let our minds play tricks on us, we often do not have the support mechanisms in place to help us to carry on. Succumbing to paranoia and hallucinations and mental debilitation can have a disastrous impact in civilian life, because it erodes trust and breeds unfounded suspicions. When we are in the hellacious periods of our lives—for example, when we think our partners, romantic or business, are cheating—we look for signs of this and begin to find evidence that the paranoia is real. In divorces we think our children are playing angles (and they may be), and our friends may be too. Giving in to either of these is bad. Patients receiving medical care doubt their caretakers, even turn on them.

For all our advances in medicine and science, the mind and its inner workings are still a mystery in many ways. We do not always understand the cause of visions or extreme paranoia. We do know, however, that when we are under extreme duress and pushed physically and mentally to our extremes, the mind will break down. We must be prepared for this and, as harsh as it sounds, be ready to ignore the insane shit we see and carry on, one paddle stroke at a time, if we hope to get out of hell.

> Most of us hallucinated during Hell Week. Don't trust what you see. Trust your brothers with you to keep you safe.
>
> —Ephraim Mattos, former Navy SEAL

If you want to survive hell, prepare to see ghosts.

Chapter 13 Lesson

Commands are often mixed with insults and mixed messages. In Hell Week, SEAL trainers who will become brothers in arms are constantly fucking with trainees, yelling insults alongside their orders. This is intentional—to make things as stressful as possible while presenting challenges that require focus. They want you to ignore and execute. This is no different than real life. A boss might be a fucking raging asshole who treats you like shit and insults you, but he also might be giving you the correct instructions that you need to execute. The key here is that some things need to get done. The volume with which you are yelled at, the abuse that is sometimes doled out—completely unfair—do not matter. Sometimes nothing at all matters but the command. Get over the insults, the humiliation, ignore them, BUT listen to what matters and do it well, even if it means lying in shit and puke and holding your breath for five seconds.

As a Navy SEAL commander and during my years running the training of SEALs and SEAL candidates, there were some instructors I had to pull back, guys who literally can go psycho when training people who they know one day may fight with them or with their brothers. You of course don't want anyone to die, but it can be good for trainers to take students to the razor's edge. In life, our inclination is to nurture. Even SEALs are this way at heart. We want to build people up. But this can be a disservice. The world is unrelenting and dangerous. You don't want a good guy leading your class during Hell Week. You want a rabid hellhound who will growl and bite and chase you every second of every day and nearly kill you, so you get stronger. You can't take this personally. You have to rise above and trust that guys like me won't let a rogue instructor kill you.

—Ryan Zinke, former Navy SEAL commander

Chapter 14 Lesson

It is no mistake that the last major training cycle during Hell Week involves simulating war. The work of a SEAL is not just to get through grueling shit, it is to get through the worst challenges, to fight through constant struggle across one hell to get to emerge on the other end to a new and more violent hell—the hell of an actual war. Ironically, if you have made it this far, you may be exhilarated by the shock and awe of the real fight. Some will hear the guns booming and rally, feeling a surge of energy. The booming gun may breathe fresh life into your soul. It also may freak you out. Whatever the case, you must be prepared for a war that may be worse and with higher stakes and challenges than you experience when you are in hell.

In civilian life, the kind of hell we sometimes face can be more debilitating than an actual war—husbands and wives who experience the unthinkable loss of a child can find themselves in the middle of the war of divorce when the strain of the loss reveals that the relationship is not as strong as it needed to be.

Just as often, after surviving a medical emergency we are confronted with the war of medical debt, a complete realignment of values and a road to full recovery that is difficult and involves rebuilding one's body. At the end of *The Iliad*, there begins *The Odyssey*.

One hell often leads to another. One war often leads to a

new war. Be ready, and if possible, after surviving one hell, let the boom of gunfire inspire you and embrace the new fight with ferocious tenacity.

> The fight only ends when you die. As long as you are physically able to continue to move, you can defeat the enemy. If you hear guns going off, you're alive and be grateful.
>
> —Ephraim Mattos, former Navy SEAL

If you want to survive hell, prepare to go to war before it ends.

Chapter 15 Lesson

Making it through Hell Week is an incredible feat, even before the pain subsides, and you are left with a feeling like no other. Pushing yourself—making life intentionally harder—is counterintuitively the way to experience the deepest and most profound joy and accomplishment. You need to recognize this. Even if you are in a zombie state you will feel it. Embrace it—you will and can grow from it, and you should be proud.

Let yourself be proud of what you accomplished and remember those who helped you through—even the bastards who tortured you along the way, like the Joker, whose torment made you stronger. No one can get you through hell but you, and you need to recognize that and acknowledge your incredible accomplishment—and yet you did not do it alone. Your parents who raised you to dare to dream, your friends who helped you along the way, your classmates, your instructors, your God, even the guys who quit helped you keep going in some ways. During your most difficult struggles, it's important to be grateful and to acknowledge the help you received along the way. The more generous you are in your gratitude, the richer you will be when you walk, limp, ride, or are carried out of hell, a free man.

Hell Week captures the very core of what drives a SEAL to beat the odds and win. Reading this book is as close to being as wet and sandy as it gets. For those of you with an interest in becoming a SEAL, do yourself a favor—if you have any doubt, read this book. If you are ready for the ultimate test and to pursue a life of adventure and service that will far exceed any dream you could possibly imagine, then you are ready for hell. Go speak to a Navy recruiter. Your new life awaits you.

—Ryan Zinke, former Navy SEAL commander